The Battle For Auschwitz

*To the memory of Rabbi Marc Tanenbaum,
who worked tirelessly to foster dialogue
and reconciliation.*

The Battle For Auschwitz

Catholic–Jewish Relations Under Strain

EMMA KLEIN

With a Foreword by Jonathan Webber

VALLENTINE MITCHELL
LONDON • PORTLAND, OR

First Published in 2001 in Great Britain by
FRANK CASS & CO. LTD.
Crown House, 47 Chase Side
Southgate, London N14 5BP

and in the United States of America by
FRANK CASS
c/o ISBS, 5804 N. E. Hassalo Street
Portland, Oregon, 97213-3644

Copyright © 2001 Emma Klein

British Library Cataloguing in Publication Data

A catalogue record for this book is available
from the British Library

ISBN 0 85303 429 X

Library of Congress Cataloguing-in-Publication Data

A catalogue record for this book is available
from the Library of Congress

Typeset by Cambridge Photosetting Services, Cambridge
Printed in Great Britain by
MPG Books Ltd, Bodmin, Cornwall

Contents

Illustrations

Foreword

There seems little doubt that identifying a universally acceptable form of commemoration at Auschwitz is one of the great challenges of our time. The immensity and utter horror of the genocide deliberately wrought during the Holocaust through the deportations and mass murders, the devastation of cultural life, and the total uprooting and dislocation of the everyday life of ordinary people – can anyone really say how these appalling historical realities can be satisfactorily represented in a museum, let alone at the site of the largest mass grave the world has ever known? Who in our generation should be charged with the moral, intellectual, and aesthetic responsibility to find a fitting memorial for such gross iniquity that would at the same time offer some wisdom and understanding, some comfort even, for the future generations of our human race?

A visitor from Mars might be forgiven for imagining that the Jewish and Christian religious leaders of our day would have succeeded in together reaching some inspired solution to the problem, in particular how to commemorate all of Auschwitz's victims in a dignified manner at the site. Unfortunately, the reality has turned out very differently. As this book documents, more than forty years after the liberation of Auschwitz an astonishing religious war of protest and mutual recrimination broke out between Jews and Christians, a war that extended itself across the world. That this should have happened at all is a sad commentary on our times. But it is a commentary that, just because of its profound relevance to the way in which we have all dealt with (or failed to deal with) this great catastrophe, deserves the widest possible readership.

Emma Klein has told the story meticulously, sparing no one. We read here of cardinals pronouncing anti-Semitic statements, of Jewish sit-ins at a convent, of Christians being accused of dejudaising the Holocaust, of rivalries between different Jewish organizations, of Christians feeling the need to defend the cross, of Jewish leaders failing to consider the consequences of their public positions, of plain ignorance, confusion, and the constant public stereotyping of others. We also read here of the fears and uncertainties involved in attempts at conflict resolution; of the sincerity of those who hold genuinely different understandings of history; of the lone voices of visionaries working for reconciliation but having difficulty maintaining their credibility with their faith communities. And we read of religion being used unashamedly to promote political interests, as well as of those who steadfastly maintain their faith in prayer as the best way to resolve human conflict.

This is, in fact, an epic story of our times, carefully pieced together by a narrator who has done her very best in treading a difficult path. The extraordinary complexity of the subject, the different points of view, the practice of impetuousness and of restraint, the misunderstandings of the parties in identifying who was the best person to speak to, the twists and turns of political negotiating, the fragility of interfaith understanding – all of these emerge clearly from the account.

As a Jewish member of the International Auschwitz Council (an advisory board appointed by the Polish government), I welcome this book. It will greatly help to explain the background to these remarkable controversies which have ignited passions very widely amongst both Jews and Christians, both inside and outside Poland. Emma Klein is a Jewish journalist who has previously published important work on Jewish issues. Her main source and sponsor in this book, which works through the Western press reports and unpublished correspondence between the religious leaders, was the distinguished London-based Jewish philanthropist Sir Sigmund Sternberg, whose own personal reputation for his contribution to Christian–Jewish dialogue worldwide, and especially Polish–Jewish relations, is well known and well deserved.

But these conflicts over Auschwitz form, unquestionably, a saddening tale, without a happy ending. In a sense, that is as it should be. As the central symbol of the Holocaust, and for Poles the central symbol of the terror of foreign occupation, Auschwitz will perhaps inevitably be plagued with contestation and dispute for a long time to come. And yet we must learn how to move forward and revise our old ways of thinking. Should we inscribe our meanings onto the site, or should we – with a greater sense of humility, perhaps – withdraw from it in silence? There is no one to tell us the final answer; but I warmly recommend this book to anyone who wants to learn how to formulate at least some of the main questions.

Jonathan Webber
Oxford, January 2001

Acknowledgements

Note on Sources

The major resource for this book was the personal archive of Sir Sigmund Sternburg, who, as the text will show, was deeply involved in the Auschwitz crisis over a number of years. I would like to thank Sir Sigmund for his help in making his archive available and for his vivid reconstruction of certain episodes through personal interview. The archive material was complemented by further personal interviews with a number of the subjects and by other source material available in England.

In preparing the book, I also consulted certain articles on the subject, most of which have been referred to in the text. I would, however, like to acknowledge Seweryn Chomet's *Outrage at Auschwitz* (London, 1990), which shed valuable light on the early stages of the conflict.

I would also like to thank Jonathan Webber, who has dedicated much of his time and expertise to Polish–Jewish relations, for his help and comments. Most particularly, I would like to acknowledge the contribution of Mrs Dorota Leviner, who made available and translated key issues of various Polish newspapers without which it would have been extremely difficult to reconstruct the latter stages of the conflict.

I believe this book has a contribution to make to the literature available on the conflict both by bringing the saga up to date and by exploring the evolution of the conflict from a source that has not previously been exposed.

Emma Klein, London, July 2000

The Polish Ambassador, Dr Stanislaw Komorowski, on behalf of the President of Poland, investing Sir Sigmund Sternberg with the Commander's Cross with a Star of the Order of Merit at the Polish Embassy, 11 October 1999.

Overview

Extracts from a Speech by the Polish Ambassador Stanislaw Komorowski, on the occasion of the Award to Sir Sigmund Sternberg of the Commander's Cross with Star of the Order of Merit of the Republic of Poland, October 1999

I would like to share with you some thoughts and quotations of Professor Bronislaw Geremek, Jan Strzlecki and Wladyslaw Bartoszewski, ideas which I find particularly important for future generations.

An intelligent witness to the horrors of World War II, a Polish resistance fighter and later a Solidarity activist, the late Jan Strzlecki once wrote that the *Endlösung* (Final Solution) was the ultimate evil because 'the very existence was reason enough for one to be killed'. He referred to wartime Poland as 'the Auschwitz catchment area'. 'We lived in the Auschwitz catchment area from which the best, richest supplies were drawn to the camp', he wrote. 'Seen from that area, the fragility of Europe was on full display ... It was just by accident that we did not ourselves dig trenches to bury tons of human ashes. Only a thin, frail partition wall separated us from a world even more cruel for the suddenness of its arrival than that from which we were separated by centuries of European history.'

And let me quote the Polish Minister of Foreign Affairs, Professor Bronislaw Geremek, who once said: 'In thinking about present-day Polish–Jewish relations, the problem of the Holocaust rises above the lingering memories of the centuries when Jews chased out of other countries of Christian Europe invariably found shelter and refuge in Poland. It is not easy to talk about Polish–Jewish relations. But talk we must, in order to overcome stereotypes, preconceptions, prejudice or downright hostility'.

An observer of Polish–Jewish relations has linked these relations to walking blindfold across a mine-field: in such circumstances, stepping on a mine is not the question of 'if' but 'when'. And, indeed, the field happens to be strewn with the well-intentioned and well-advised casualties from both sides. However, undeterred, a new man ventures out across the mine-field in the belief that the risk is worth taking because the objective is worth achieving. And so it goes on. For the sake of shedding bias and gaining a wealth of insight and knowledge.

More than any other event in the long and difficult Polish–Jewish history, the murder of Jews by Germans in Poland remains its defining event. It is, indeed, one of the most important events of our civilisation as a whole. And this remains true regardless of the fact that not only the victims are gone, but also that of the few surviving victims, eye-witnesses to and perpetrators of the crime, none will be around in the not-too-distant future.

Auschwitz, Treblinka and the Warsaw ghetto indelibly marked us all. Still, we do have a future. We – Poles and Jews – do have a future together. Not only because there are but a few nations more aware than ourselves of the basic fact that our future is not guaranteed, that we cannot relent in our efforts to secure it for our people. Before the enemy was defeated, Poland had been struck off the map of Europe and the Jewish people had been singled out for industrial-scale annihilation. Although the two kinds of suffering are hardly identical, they give us a shared awareness denied to happier nations. Our shared commitment to democracy and human rights stems from that awareness.

That commitment also involves the need to honestly face up to our past, to come to terms with it and to work for a different, happier future. This means coming round to accept by the Polish side that anti-Semitism – which was first introduced into Poland by the Russian tsarist authorities but had grown strong and deep native roots by the time Poland regained its independence in the early twentieth century – that anti-Semitism was an important element of contemporary Jewish experience. The Jews, especially in inter-war Poland, were regarded as aliens by a large segment of Polish society. And they knew it. But when the Germans invaded bringing with them the unspeakable horrors of the *Shoah*, most Jews felt abandoned and even betrayed by society at large. It will be remembered that the largest number of trees at Yad Vashem have been planted in honour of the Poles who saved Jewish lives, but, as Wladyslaw Bartoszewski once correctly put it, 'only those did enough who gave their own lives'.

Democratic Poland acknowledges the evils of the past because we have an obligation to our citizens and to the truth. Doing the right thing requires no ulterior motive. That is also why we shall be uncompromising in our reactions to any manifestations of anti-Semitism in Poland. We shall denounce Holocaust denials and condemn speeches filled with hate. In so doing, we shall be bound by the spirit and letter of the law, but also, let's face it, limited by a certain reluctance of law-enforcement officials to prosecute what they regard as nothing more than 'thought crime'. The Catholic Church, which was first to recognize its past record in respect of its attitude towards the Jews, has made tremendous efforts to make up for the past. It has been organizing annual days of teaching about Judaism, offering guidance to parish priests. Unfortunately, not all of the priests choose to follow that guidance.

Polish–Jewish co-operation needs to be an ongoing process. The evil of anti-Semitism cannot be relativized. Yet we hope that as the Poles review and reject their own bias, they will not be alone in doing so. We have all heard pronouncements about 'Poles suckling anti-Semitism with their mothers' milk', about 'Polish concentration camps', about 'the accursed country' – meaning Poland. Prejudice and bias are invariably shameful wherever they occur. Knowing how hard it is to reform attitudes on our own side of the divide, we do not expect miracles on the other. But we do expect more efforts to be made, and credit given where it is due. For it is the right thing to do.

Ten years ago my country was emerging from a long night that lasted half a century. Few would have expected it soon to become a stable and thriving democracy, secure for the first time in its recent history through membership of NATO, forward-looking and full of hope. Fewer people, I am sure, would have expected Poland's current tiny Jewish community to experience the rebirth and growth it has undergone. But very few indeed would have seen develop a Polish–Jewish partnership of interest, as seen in the thriving state of our relations with Israel and with Diaspora communities abroad, and in our shared values and aspirations. This is a huge common success, and I want once again to thank Sir Sigmund Sternberg for having played a very important part.

It might still be a mine-field, but, because of you, Sir Sigmund, and many others like you, we are no longer blindfold and have a common map. Let us then walk together in the same direction.

1. 1984–86:
A Convent at Auschwitz – Shrine or Desecration?

The name 'Auschwitz' still conjures up memories of the greatest atrocity perpetrated in a century marked by unprecedented levels of violence, savagery and destruction. The mass murder camp where some 1.1 million people, 90 per cent of them Jews,* were systematically gassed to death, Auschwitz is branded in the consciousness of most Jews as the horrific culmination of two millennia of persecution and martyrdom. Before the Wannsee conference of 1942, however, which put the finishing touches to Hitler's plans for the 'Final Solution to the Jewish question', the concentration camp at Auschwitz had been earmarked by the Nazis for the incarceration and slaughter of Soviet prisoners of war and leaders of the Polish establishment, aristocracy and intelligentsia, among whom were many members of the Resistance, both Polish and Jewish. In 1979 the Polish government and the World Jewish Congress, a New York-based organization, agreed that Auschwitz should be placed on the UNESCO World Heritage List as a site of genocide.

On 1 August 1984, almost 40 years after the camp was liberated, a group of some 15 Carmelite nuns took over a building adjacent to the walls of the concentration camp. Known as 'the old theatre', the building had been used to store the Zyklon B poison utilized in the gas chambers. At the request of Cardinal Franciszek Macharski, Archbishop of the Cracow diocese, the nuns had been granted a 99-year lease by the local authorities and at the end of September a declaration was made by high-ranking members of the Polish Church, voicing approval of the establishment of the convent at Auschwitz. The Church officials, who included Macharski, had no inkling at the time of the tinderbox their decision had set alight.

On the contrary, viewed from a Catholic perspective, the desire of the nuns to pray for the expiation of the crimes committed in Auschwitz and to obtain by intercession the mercy of God seemed to reflect Christian goodwill and solidarity towards the suffering of the Jewish people. How

* The latest figure provided by the Auschwitz Museum – though 'approximately 1.5 million' appears on the monument at Birkenau.

were Catholics to know that in contrast to their own need to venerate and make sacred a site of martyrdom, Jewish tradition deems it fit to shun such a spot and leave it desolate? The gap in the two religious perspectives was feelingly articulated by no less a figure than Archbishop Muszynski of Gniezno who, as Monseigneur Muszynski, was to head the Polish Commission for Christian–Jewish dialogue for ten years:

> I would never have expected that the Jews would react in such a way. We thought that first of all, it's the same God. I expected that believing Jews would have more or less the same feelings. I was very much surprised that the Jews had something against the nuns who were engaged in silent prayer in this place. We didn't know each other, we didn't have any contact with each other.

The fact that earlier, smaller-scale initiatives to pray for the murdered and their oppressors had received a positive reaction from Polish Jews served to reinforce the Catholic position. And certainly, in the early days at least, the Carmelite convent at Auschwitz did not disturb the small Polish–Jewish community, as a prominent activist, Dr Stanislaw Krajewski, confirms. A member of the International Council of the Auschwitz–Birkenau Museum, Krajewski pointed out that the convent building was not part of the itinerary for visitors to Auschwitz: 'I saw that the convent was in an abandoned building just outside the camp base. I was and would have been satisfied with it had I been sure that it wouldn't have grown.'

Although the Carmelites are an enclosed order, the convent soon became an integral part of the many Cracow coach tours visiting the Auschwitz section of the Auschwitz–Birkenau complex known as the Museum of Martyrdom. It came to the attention of the outside world in May 1985 after the Belgian branch of an organization known as 'Aid to the Church in Need' issued a bulletin appealing for funds to help the nuns adapt and repair the convent building. Distributed shortly before Pope John Paul II was due to visit the Benelux countries, the bulletin spoke of the convent at Auschwitz as 'a gift for the Pope', who, it was later claimed, had proposed the idea for the convent when he was Archbishop of Cracow. The suggestion that the convent was to be 'a spiritual fortress' and 'a guarantee of the conversion of stray brothers' can be seen as particularly provocative.

While the latter sentiments might arguably have been directed at the numerous Poles who had embraced atheism under the communist regime, the prayer for 'the conversion of the perfidious Jews' had long been a standard part of Catholic liturgy. The publication in 1965 of the Vatican II document, *Nostra Aetate*, did, indeed, call for a radical review of Catholic perceptions of Jews and some of its tenets had been embraced by an enlightened Western Catholic élite. However it is likely that the influence of *Nostra Aetate* would have been less far-reaching among the Catholic hierarchies of Eastern Europe.

The triumphalist tone of the Belgian bulletin and its notable omission of any reference to Auschwitz as a place where numerous European Jewish communities had been annihilated hardly endeared the cause it was promoting to the Jewish world. Reactions to the convent were first heard from Jewish organizations in the Francophone countries and shortly afterwards from other parts of Europe, from Israel and from the USA. Jews engaged in Christian–Jewish dialogue were, on the whole, muted in their response. Rabbi David Rosen of the Anti-Defamation League is one example:

> The ADL didn't want to make a thing of it. Their attitude was, it is not as if there are Jews there at the time who are involved in it and it's not as if it's actually on the property itself. By making a big thing, you're basically trying to go to war with the Catholic Church.

During the latter months of 1985, however, the majority of Jewish voices, led by the influential World Jewish Congress (WJC), were raised in sharp objection. Rosen sees the WJC's role as pivotal:

> To some extent the WJC did determine the tune. Their style created the atmosphere in which no public Jewish organization could not get involved. Had the WJC not got involved, those issues might not have developed in the way they did.

The hue and cry came as a surprise to Krajewski and other Polish Jews who remembered that there had been no protests at the way the communist regime had virtually obliterated the role of the Jews as the principal victims of the mass murder camp. This is vividly confirmed by the film-maker Mira Hamermesh, who reports on a pilgrimage to Auschwitz in 1959: 'In the official communist version, all the victims were martyrs of anti-fascist resistance. The guide never mentioned Jews.'

Forgetful, or perhaps ignorant, of the fact that Poles saw Auschwitz as a focal point of their own suffering and martyrdom under the Nazis, Jewish protesters saw no justification for the presence of the Carmelites. They were affronted at what was perceived as an attempt not merely to dejudaise but to 'Christianize' the vast Jewish graveyard that Auschwitz had become. Among the protesters were survivors of the Holocaust who, not surprisingly, were particularly offended. As Rosen points out: 'Once it had become a big issue, then you couldn't keep quiet any longer.'

A few prominent Jews were initially indifferent to the presence of the nuns at Auschwitz. One was Sir Sigmund Sternberg, a British businessman and philanthropist of Hungarian origin. Appointed in 1979 as Chairman of the Executive of the International Council of Christians and Jews, an umbrella organization embracing Christian–Jewish networks in more than 30 countries, he had spent much of his time and energy assiduously cultivating improved relations with the Catholic world and was a firm believer in dialogue. While on a subliminal level he remained traumatized by the destruction of the bulk of Hungarian Jewry in a matter of months in 1944, when the allies were already aware of the implications of the 'Final Solution', he was always conscious of his own good fortune in having left Nazi Europe in time. On a gut level, then, the convent at Auschwitz was not offensive to him – 'it didn't bother me personally, it didn't bother me very much' – particularly as the building itself was outside the perimeters of the camp.

But if he had attuned himself to be sensitive to the feelings of his partners in dialogue, how much more so was he to the distress of his co-religionists who had survived the *Shoah*:

> The convent started bothering me when the survivors were upset by it. But I must be careful, I'm not in a position to judge because I've not been in the Holocaust. Obviously these people were outraged, people who were survivors. And if they felt bad about it, of course it started bothering me.

The same year, 1985, brought Sternberg recognition for his efforts to build bridges with the Catholic world. He was appointed Knight Commander of the Papal Equestrian Order of St Gregory, one of the few Jews to have been honoured in this way by the Vatican. Catholic friends and acquaintances have pointed out that in conferring this award on Sternberg, the Vatican was making a gesture of friendship towards the Jews. Another, more conspicuous gesture was John Paul II's visit to the Rome synagogue in April 1986, where Sternberg accompanied him in full Papal Knight's regalia.

Whether it was mere chance that Sternberg's elevation coincided with circumstances which were threatening the goodwill that had been painstakingly built up between representatives of the two faith communities is open to question. The growth of trust between Jews and Catholics had started gradually in the aftermath of the Second World War when a few farsighted clergymen felt the need to make amends for what was perceived as the Church's less than glorious role during the Holocaust; it had been accelerated by conciliatory voices and gestures at the Second Vatican Council set up by Pope John XXIII in the early 1960s. Now these hard-won developments were being threatened by the row simmering over the presence of the nuns at Auschwitz.

2. July 1986–February 1989:
Attempts at Resolution

To defuse the controversy, fuelled by protests and demonstrations throughout the world not only by Jews but also by sympathetic Christians, a Catholic–Jewish summit meeting took place in Geneva on 22 July 1986. Cardinal Macharski, accompanied by Fr Stanislaw Musial, Secretary of the Polish Church's Commission for Dialogue with Judaism, and Jerzy Turowicz, editor of the Catholic weekly *Tygodnik Powszechny*, joined three Western cardinals, the Belgian primate Cardinal Gottfried Danneels, Cardinal Albert Decourtray, Archbishop of Lyons and Chairman of the French Bishops' Conference, and the Archbishop of Paris, Cardinal Jean-Marie Lustiger, a converted Jew. The Jewish delegation was led by Théo Klein, President of CRIF, the representative Council of Jewish Organizations in France. He was accompanied by his Belgian and Italian counterparts, Markus Pardes and Tullia Zevi respectively, and by French Chief Rabbi René-Samuel Sirat and Professor Ady Steg.

At the meeting, which lasted one day, Macharski undertook to halt further construction of the convent while discussions continued. A joint communiqué was published recognizing 'the uncontested realities of the symbolic character of the extermination camp of Auschwitz, monument and memory of the Holocaust' and pledging a continuation of dialogue. At the same time the participants had drafted the Auschwitz Declaration, beginning with the Hebrew word *Zakhor*–Remember. The declaration recognized Auschwitz and Birkenau as symbols of the Final Solution but also remembered the others – Poles, Russians and Gypsies – who had been murdered in Auschwitz.

Seven months later, on 22 February 1987, a second meeting was held in Geneva when the original participants were joined by additional delegates from both sides. The most prominent addition to the Jewish delegation was Dr Gerhart Riegner, the veteran co-chairman of the Governing Board of the WJC. Riegner was also to receive a Papal Knighthood in recognition of his many years of work in the field of Christian–Jewish relations.

After lengthy discussions, a communiqué was issued, reiterating the previous Geneva declaration and proposing that a Centre for Information, Education, Meeting and Prayer should be built some 500 metres outside the Auschwitz–Birkenau concentration camps. It was hoped that the centre would be used for conferences between Christians and Jews, as a resource to combat 'revisionism' and disinformation about the Holocaust and to provide further information for visitors to the camp. Most significantly, the establishment of the new centre implied 'that the Carmelites' prayer initiative will find in this new context its rightful place, its confirmation and its true meaning'.

Essentially, then, as seen in the Western world, the Geneva accords of 1987 committed the Polish Church to relocating the Carmelites within the confines of the proposed new conference centre, well outside the camp. The deadline agreed was 21 February 1989, only two years away. While reactions to the accord were mixed, one less than enthusiastic voice stood out. This was the Polish primate, Cardinal Jozef Glemp, who stated bluntly that 'the dialogue between the Jews and Catholics must continue. This matter is not terminated'. With hindsight it is easy to ask why Glemp's presence was not deemed indispensable to the Geneva deliberations.

This is certainly Sternberg's view. 'They should really have negotiated with Cardinal Glemp. He was the primate of Poland,' he often reiterates. It later became clear that Glemp resented having been left out of the discussions about the Carmelites. Sternberg, in contrast, had no interest in getting involved in the dispute at that stage. 'I left it to the others. Too many people were negotiating and I didn't believe they were going to get anywhere and I didn't want to get involved in their negotiations.' His scepticism was twofold. 'My belief is when too many people negotiate, usually nothing happens. The art is really to find the right person who can make decisions. They were not negotiating with the right person.'

Unsurprisingly, there was not much movement on the Polish front. No doubt the period prescribed by the Geneva accords may have been unrealistic, given the time needed to prepare plans for the proposed centre and have them approved, let alone find funds for the project. Moreover, the so-called 'accords' were seen by prominent churchmen in Poland as no more than a declaration of intent. According to Archbishop Muszynski, it was only once the centre was built that any agreement for the transfer of the nuns could be reached. Moreover, the 'accords' were legally untenable, as Muszynski explained:

> From the point of view of Canon Law, cardinals cannot make an agreement on behalf of another diocese. While the Jews would

consider a pact achieved with four cardinals as a very important
agreement, in Canon Law it was very questionable.

The impracticality of expecting the sisters to move before alternative accommodation was built for them in the new centre was pointed
out by the Superior General of the Carmelite Order, Father Phillipe
Sainz de Baranda, in a letter to Théo Klein, a co-president of the second Geneva meeting. Writing on 9 February 1989, barely two weeks
before the February deadline, Father Sainz de Baranda emphasized
his order's support for the implementation of the Geneva declarations,
'signed by eminent representatives of the Church in Europe'. 'The
Carmelites of Auschwitz must accept the planned move to install themselves in the new convent as soon as the latter is built,' he wrote, adding
that his position had been made known to the sisters at Auschwitz,
'who accepted it fully'. However, Sainz de Baranda stated clearly, in the
meantime the sisters would remain where they were at present, 'in
the old theatre now converted into a convent'. He urged that the new
convent be built as soon as possible in the hope that relations between
Jews and Christians 'suffer no new tensions because of Auschwitz'.

Father Sainz de Baranda's expectations may be seen as somewhat
sanguine, particularly as yet another factor was instrumental in holding matters up. As Archbishop Luigi Barbarito, the then Papal Nuncio in London pointed out, 'It was still the communist government at
the time. The Church and the government didn't agree and the government had some interest in harassing the Church and putting it on
the spot.' With the deadline of 22 February 1989 passing without any
building works having commenced at the site of the centre, a new
deadline for the departure of the nuns was set by the Catholic negotiators at Geneva for 22 July the same year.

The announcement was welcomed by Rabbi Marc Tanenbaum, international consultant for the American Jewish Committee and an experienced exponent of Christian–Jewish dialogue. Designated in a national
poll as 'one of the ten most influential and respected religious leaders
in America', Tanenbaum's weekly commentaries and radio broadcasts
reached hundreds of thousands of readers and listeners. Writing in the
West Coast Jewish News, he sought to present a balanced picture of the
current situation by suggesting to his readers that 'most Jews understand the appropriateness of their [the Carmelites'] honouring Polish
Catholic victims of Nazism'. However, since 'Auschwitz was built for
the primary purpose of exterminating European Jews', the convent
had become 'a gesture of appropriation rather than an act of reconciliation'. The new deadline to move the convent to the proposed centre
was, Tanenbaum believed, 'a constructive move in the right direction'.

3. February–July 1989:
The Slide towards Confrontation

The February date was marked in a very different way at the site of the convent at Auschwitz. It was then that the large wooden cross, some seven metres high, was erected in the centre of the lawn of the convent garden. As the French journal, *Libération*, reported five months later: 'On 22 February, the 15 Polish sisters, far from moving, were fitting out the place in a manner that was anything but provisional and were putting up, at the gate of the camp, a wooden cross seven metres high.' This was the cross which had been used for the mass John Paul II had said at Birkenau ten years earlier. The spot where it now stood marked the gravel ditch where Polish resistance fighters were shot early on in the history of the Auschwitz concentration camp.

If the cross at Auschwitz can be seen to have tremendous significance for the Carmelites themselves and, by extension, for many Catholic Poles, it constituted an undeniable provocation to most Jews. In fact, as a report in *Le Monde* of 18 July pointed out, 'this new business of the cross puts the whole matter of the convent in second place'. Krajewski, too, found the cross unacceptable:

> To me it was certainly much more of a problem. It was and is much more of a problem than the convent itself because the cross is visible and it really tries to dominate the space over the camp and, in fact, it does.

According to other objective observers, the cross does, in fact, dominate one of the two access roads to the entrance to the camp.

What is fascinating, however, is that both Krajewski and Waldemar Chrostowski of the Polish Academy of Catholic Theology date the erection of the cross to the autumn of 1989. Krajewski recalls that 'the cross came in the heat of the controversy in 1989, when the religious war was full on. It was at the peak of the religious war'. He stresses that it was put up after some controversial Jewish protests at the site of the convent that summer and after Cardinal Glemp had reacted to the protests with allegations that appeared to contain anti-Semitic stereotypes.

Chrostowski, in a document about the Auschwitz convent controversy, states that 'in autumn 1989 a big cross was erected close by the
Carmeliten [sic] nuns' convent' and goes on to discuss the implications.
While recognizing that, for many Jews, 'the appearance of the cross
was a new manifestation of the "christianization" of Auschwitz', he
points out that from the perspective of many Catholics, 'defence of the
cross' became a priority and cites the words of Rev. Anastasy Gegotek:
'The departure of the nuns from this place would mean for them the
renouncing of the Cross, that is the renouncing of their faith.'

In 1989 the Iron Curtain was fast disappearing. Nevertheless it was
early enough in the new era for a process of disinformation to have
continued, thereby causing both Krajewski and Chrostowski, who were
based in Warsaw, to remain ignorant of a development that was widely
and freely reported throughout the Western world. Indeed a group of
Jews from the Manor House Society in London visiting Auschwitz in
April that year commented that 'the huge wooden cross visible from
most parts of the camp was the last straw'.

It is possible, of course, that Chrostowski's dating of the cross was
part of the campaign of disinformation. The implications are obvious.
For Poles, the cross was put up in defiant reaction to unseemly Jewish
protests, whereas in fact it was one of the causes that fuelled those
same protests. What the nuns at Auschwitz and their supporters were
defying when the cross was put up on 22 February 1989 was the original
deadline of the Geneva accord. Raising the cross was a declaration by
the Carmelites vowed to silence that they were there to stay.

As the months passed, there was no reason to believe that the new,
July deadline would prove any more effective than the one it had
replaced. With the implementation of the Geneva accords in jeopardy,
hostile noises and threats of action were beginning to be heard from
organizations throughout the Jewish world. The World Jewish Congress, for one, was calling for world Jewry to boycott meetings with the
Pope, a 'melodramatic gesture' condemned by Tanenbaum as 'absurd,
mischievous and counterproductive'.

In an op-ed article in the *Jewish Exponent* in May, Tanenbaum explained
his reasons for dissociating himself from the boycott resolution, pointing out that the key Catholic authorities in Europe, including the
Pope, had 'agreed in writing several times to remove the convent from
the grounds of Auschwitz'. He recalled, too, the 'remarkable sensitivity'
to Jewish feelings shown by Catholic leaders, including Vatican representatives, with whom he had negotiated as chairman of the International Jewish Committee on Interreligious Consultations (IJCIC),
an umbrella group of Jewish organizations established to carry on a
dialogue with the Vatican and other religious bodies. The article went

on to acknowledge the practical problem of finding 'an interim place of domicile' for the Carmelites until the new centre was built and to urge Jewish leaders to continue to press for assurances that the interim move would, indeed, take place. Nevertheless, the boycott was seen as particularly inappropriate in view of the Pope's sympathy with the Jewish stance on the convent issue.

Although, on the official level, the Vatican had maintained a judicious silence about the convent, regarding it as a matter for the local diocese to deal with, the Holy See was well aware of the potential damage to which the dispute could give rise and had communicated its stance on the Geneva declaration through diplomatic channels. Indeed, the Pontiff had, himself, voiced support for the proposed new centre in an address to the Jewish community of Vienna the previous year when he had expressed the hope that the centre might produce 'fruitful results' and 'serve as a model for other nations'.

While belligerent rumblings continued, endangering Catholic–Jewish relations, Sternberg advocated calm diplomacy. Speaking in June at a meeting of the Board of Deputies of British Jews, he urged caution. 'Only the Catholic Church in Poland has the power to move the convent,' he said. 'Wise, calm negotiations would be more effective than noisy protests.' In a private letter to an American-Jewish leader, he pointed out that it was pointless to assist 'those elements in the Church and elsewhere which are hostile to us by giving them a "cause" more attractive to and more comprehensible to the media than ours'. Sternberg's warnings, however, were not appreciated by the recipients of the letter. Even within Anglo-Jewry, a call was made by the Board of Deputies for prayers to be recited in synagogues for the removal of the convent.

It was at that point that Sternberg decided to take a more proactive line. He contacted the prioresses at two Carmelite monasteries in England with whom he had been in correspondence for some time. Although the prioresses shared his concern that their sisters at Auschwitz were 'presenting a stumbling block' to relations between Jews and Christians, they could offer no practical advice beyond faith in the power of prayer.

Tanenbaum, too, was becoming increasingly preoccupied with the rapidly deteriorating situation. Sitting at his typewriter early in July to prepare an op-ed article for the *New York Times*, he reviewed the convent controversy from all angles. His notes reveal the anguished soul-searching of a scrupulously fair man struggling to do justice to conflicting perspectives without in any way compromising his own passionately held beliefs.

Tanenbaum was in communication with the then Bishop Henryk Muszynski, the leading proponent of Catholic–Jewish dialogue in

Poland, and felt obliged to acknowledge his predicament. 'I am not able to see how to convince in a plausible way my compatriots that the Carmelite convent should be moved at once to a not yet existing "interim centre",' Muszynski had written. Nevertheless, Tanenbaum's patience with the Catholic position was becoming severely strained. 'Despite their [the Carmelites'] pious intentions their presence has generated endless misunderstanding which is now turning to ill will,' he mused, recognizing that the issue had become 'a make-or-break test for Christian–Jewish relations' and 'challenged the sincerity of a far wider group than those directly concerned with the Auschwitz Carmelites'. He recognized, too, that 'from the Jewish point of view Christian–Jewish relations are only worth fostering if over a critical issue like this they can deliver satisfaction'.

Tanenbaum had been involved in Christian–Jewish dialogue for 30 years and had the distinction of being the only rabbi present as a guest observer at the Second Vatican Council. Fair-minded and knowledgeable as he was with regard to Catholic beliefs, his deepest empathy was with the millennial suffering of his co-religionists:

> To the Jews of Europe, Christianity was not a religion of the love of God but a religion of hostility towards the Jews. A Christian chapel in Auschwitz, now topped by a cross, feels to them like an attempt to hound the dead even beyond the grave – or even to celebrate Jewish extermination as a kind of Christian triumph.

Striving to balance two totally contradictory approaches which had hidden the fact that 'each side in its own way is trying to express its utmost sorrow and grief', the rabbi concluded that:

> Auschwitz is the last place on earth at which Jews can be expected to look on Christian symbolism with sympathy. And it is the Christians who must give way – for they were not only among the victims; they were among the murderers.

As a contemplative man of wide-ranging vision, Tanenbaum perceived that the current conflict bore more complex implications:

> Embedded in this tangled web are competing and conflicting self-perceptions of Jews, Roman Catholics, Poles and other national groups; vastly different understandings of history, still unreconciled views of how the victims of Nazism should be memorialized.

Tanenbaum's appreciation of the complexity of the situation was shared by the Oxford academic Jonathan Webber, who went much further than the rabbi in expounding a controversial and strikingly original perspective on the Auschwitz imbroglio. A social scientist who was to become a fellow of the Jagiellonian University of Cracow and a founder member of the International Auschwitz Council, Webber, an orthodox Jew, took the view that the Carmelites should stay at Auschwitz, partly for the reason that they contributed a spiritual dimension to the understanding of the Holocaust. More important, however, was his emphasis on the need for some Jewish shrine or memorial to be established at Auschwitz as an educational and spiritual resource for future generations. This would not, he believed, be provided by the proposed new centre. These observations were put forward in a letter published in the *Jewish Chronicle* on 14 July and generated a great deal of correspondence.

Webber's was, of course, a minority view. And with the July deadline imminent, Sternberg, ever the practical man, realized that some gesture from Poland was needed. Accordingly, on 10 July he wrote to Dr Zbigniew Gertych, the Polish ambassador in London, suggesting that the Polish government make an offer of temporary accommodation for the Auschwitz Carmelites pending the building of the new convent. The offer could be made in a statement or in an open letter to Sternberg. At the same time he declared himself willing to go to Poland to help negotiate the acquisition of interim premises, together with Tanenbaum.

4. July–September 1989:
Religious War

It was too late, however, to calm the continuing frustration in some Jewish quarters which was fast reaching boiling point. The initiative was seized by a man whose course of action was diametrically opposed to anything Sternberg or Tanenbaum would have prescribed. Rabbi Avi Weiss from Riverdale in the Bronx would seem an unlikely aggressor, as some have portrayed him. Clean-shaven and mild-mannered, he was a disciple of the 'hippy' rabbi, the late Shlomo Carlebach, and is given to playing the guitar, preaching peace and love and conducting services in a 'happy-clappy' fashion. With quite a following among American orthodox Jews, he is particularly admired by women for his attempts to include them as much as possible in Jewish ritual. An observer who attended a seminar given by him at the end of 1997 commented on the gentleness of his approach but could imagine that he was capable of great anger.

On 14 July 1989, a group of seven American Jews led by Weiss arrived at the gates of the convent. It was anger at what he perceived as an attempt to 'Christianize the Holocaust' that propelled Weiss to Auschwitz. The events that ensued, which have been interpreted in any number of ways, brought the convent imbroglio back to the headlines.

According to a notably objective Polish reporter, Anna Husarka, writing in the Solidarity newspaper *Gazeta Wyborcza*, the Jews rang the bell, wishing to explain to the sisters why they were there – although they could not speak Polish – and continued ringing and trying to attract the nuns' attention. Failing to receive any response, the seven men then scaled the fence and found themselves in the courtyard of the convent. They knocked on the wooden door of the convent but once again failed to get a response. It was Friday afternoon and they put on their prayer shawls, sat down, lit Shabbat candles, blew rams' horns and brought out their Bibles.

Another report, in *Le Monde*, mentions that the demonstrators brandished a banner inscribed in Polish, 'Sisters, do not pray for the Jewish martyrs. They were not Christian.' While his followers chanted prayers, Weiss read a declaration condemning the Holy See for authorizing the establishment of the convent to a group of journalists and onlookers standing in front of the convent. He then requested that the Polish ecclesiastical authorities at least remove the huge wooden cross, as an initial gesture of good will.

Reported this way, Weiss and his followers were engaged in nothing more than a peaceful if hardly silent demonstration. While such behaviour might have aroused little comment in America or the West in general, it was obviously perceived quite differently in an Eastern-bloc country where free demonstrations were not run-of-the-mill. Moreover, eyebrows may well be raised at the presence, in a courtyard of an enclosed convent of nuns vowed to silence, of seven strange men, whether they were engaged in non-violent verbal protest or in some sort of prayer with their heads covered. An outlandish way of going about things, no doubt, but violent it was not.

Before long, however, some Poles engaged in building works appeared at the windows of the convent, jeered at the Jews and demanded that they leave the convent. Then they drenched Weiss and his followers with buckets of water mixed with cement, according to some French newspaper reports – or mixed with paint and urine, according to Weiss. Finally they dragged the Jews out by force. Outside, while bystanders, including policemen and a priest looked on, the workers punched and kicked the Jews and shouted obscenities.

Two days later, according to *Le Monde*, Weiss and his followers tried in vain to issue a protest to Cardinal Macharski in Cracow; they were warned that if such a shameful incident should occur again, the Polish Church would report it to the international tribunal at The Hague. Undaunted, the Americans returned to the convent garden, wearing the striped pyjamas of concentration camp inmates. They were joined by a group of 30 Canadian Jews who remained outside the convent.

The following Sunday a large group of Belgian Jewish students demonstrated outside the convent and a day later a group of former camp inmates led by the emeritus Chief Rabbi of France, René-Samuel Sirat, did so. In Paris representatives of Jewish youth organizations demonstrated outside the fence of the Apostolic Nuncio using the emotive slogan 'Pas de croix sur nos cendres' – 'No cross over our ashes'.

What Krajewski refers to as 'the religious wars' had begun. Even moderate voices in the Jewish world, particularly in America, were outraged at the treatment meted out to Weiss and his followers. While deploring the action Weiss had taken, Théo Klein, the leader of the Jewish delegation to the Geneva talks, called for a freeze in Catholic–Jewish relations. His successor as president of CRIF, Jean Kahn, was more outspoken. 'The Carmelites' vow is to join in their prayers victims and executioners,' he declared at a ceremony commemorating a noto-rious round-up of French Jews by the Nazis, 'This mixture in a place where the sky was silent while our people were being massacred is unacceptable to us.'

Ironically, as Anna Husarka made clear in an intriguing and in-sightful report for *The Washington Post*, one of the main problems with the Weiss initiative was 'a failure to understand'. 'Things went much better on the two occasions when the group's leader, Rabbi Avraham Weiss, was able to get round the language barrier and speak with the Poles,' Husarka wrote. 'He had a courteous exchange with the secretary of the Cracow bishopric. The rabbi spoke Yiddish, the priest German.'

What was desperately needed to take the heat out of the situation was dialogue. This was something Sternberg, for one, understood only too well. In his letter of 10 July to Dr Gertych he had warned that a breakdown of dialogue could result in a resurgence of anti-Semitism 'all over the world [and] especially in Poland, which would be extremely damaging to the country'. The Weiss escapade had intervened before there could be any reaction to his proposal of temporary accommodation for the Carmelites.

On 25 July, however, a statement was issued by the Polish govern-ment expressing interest in 'the initiation of peaceful and honest action for the implementation of the Geneva agreement as soon as possible'. The statement voiced concern at the recent protests at the convent and gave some details of approvals sought for the site of the centre proposed in the Geneva accords, the earliest being in March 1989, the month after the original deadline for the nuns' move had expired. Since the centre had not been built, however, the convent had to remain on the present site.

Significantly, there was no mention of temporary accommodation, as Sternberg pointed out in another letter to Dr Gertych, which he urged the ambassador to forward to General Jaruzelski, the Polish Prime Minister. He reiterated his suggestion that he and Tanenbaum be invited to Poland to speak personally to Jaruzelski.

Up to this point, Sternberg had exploited his good relations with the Polish ambassador to push for some demonstration of goodwill from the Polish government. It was then that he received a request from another quarter. Archbishop Luigi Barbarito, the Papal Nuncio in London, was worried by 'the deteriorating aspect of events', particu-larly after the Weiss incursion which in many newspapers was portrayed more as an 'assault'. 'To prevent this escalation from reaching a point of no return, I said to Sir Sigmund, "It's better that you deal directly with the Catholic hierarchy in Poland. When you can talk, dialogue and explain the reason and also if you can offer some help, this would be far more acceptable.'"

Since Sternberg was not acquainted with Cardinal Macharski and had only a nodding acquaintance with the Polish primate he was initially hesitant. But Barbarito, boosted by the fact that some months earlier the primate had called at the *nunciatura* on his way to Ireland, was able to reassure him that he would write a letter of introduction. In it, the Nuncio asked the Polish cardinals to receive Sternberg and Tanenbaum, together with Bishop Gerald Mahon from the Westminster Archdiocese, who was closely involved in dialogue.

Sternberg was quick to put the letter to use. On 9 August he sent a two-page telex to Macharski, reiterating the need for a 'temporary building' which would be purpose-built. On a practical level he indicated that finance for the building might be forthcoming from the Catholic Bishops' Conference in Bonn and suggested a meeting on the site with a group of key figures including the mayor of Auschwitz, the engineer in charge of the proposed building works for the centre, an architect from Germany, a representative of the German Catholic Church and one of the Carmelite nuns. To add weight to his proposal he mentioned that he and other officers of the Council of Christians and Jews would be having an audience with the Pope the following month, coinciding with celebrations for the eightieth birthday of Cardinal Johannes Willebrands, President of the Vatican Commission for Relations with Judaism, 'a joyous event ... which should not be marred by anything that would detract from the occasion'.

This was combined with a warning. The European Jewish Congress (EJC), which Sternberg would be attending, was to be held in London the following month and, unless his proposals for settling the convent situation were heeded, a resolution would be drafted condemning those who were breaking the agreement. As a final twist to his arguments, he assured Macharski that in considering 'this unique proposition', the cardinal would not be seen as having given in to pressure, since it was on record that Sternberg and Tanenbaum had been discussing the matter well before the latest developments. 'At one stroke you will take the heat out of the situation and remove the tension,' he concluded.

In taking his case to the highest echelons of the Polish Church, Sternberg was laying his credentials as a Papal Knight on the line. Obviously, many Poles were smarting from the incidents of the previous month. Despite the high level of objectivity and neutrality with which these had been reported in the Polish press as a whole – more so, incidentally, than in the English press, which tended to portray Weiss and his associates as 'hotheads' or 'fanatics' who had 'physically assaulted' the Carmelites and 'tried to remove them by force or even

kill them' – the official Polish Press Agency and various Church organs
had used much more emotive language, describing the Jews as 'invading'
the convent grounds with 'brutal shouting' and 'threatening behaviour'.

In what appears to be an incredible coincidence of timing, Sternberg's
telex was pipped to the post by a statement issued by Macharski on
8 August. It was the first definitive Catholic counter-charge in the
'religious wars'. In essence, the cardinal was backing down from the
commitment he had made at Geneva to oversee the building of the
Centre for Information, Education, Meetings and Prayer which was to
incorporate a new home for the Auschwitz Carmelites, a project for
which, he claimed, he had entertained the highest hopes. He justified
his decision by excoriating the 'violent campaign of accusation and
slander' the delay in the implementation of the 'unrealistic deadline'
for the construction of the Centre had fomented in Western Jewish
circles and the 'offensive aggression, which is not merely verbal' which
had 'found an echo in Auschwitz'.

Amid the hostile reactions provoked by Macharski's statement was
Sternberg's three-page telex dated 14 August. It is possible he may
not have been aware that the cardinal's statement predated his earlier
communication. Sternberg professed himself 'devastated' by the stance
Macharski had taken which implied, in effect, that the Carmelites
would not move and warned that the consequences for Catholic–Jewish
relations were 'unimaginable'. Taking issue with Macharski's alle-
gation that the only voice calling for self-control was that of Jewish
organizations in Poland, he produced a list of Jewish dignatories and
organizations, from the then Chief Rabbi Lord Jacobovits downwards,
who deplored the demonstrations at Auschwitz and went on to cite a
passage from a letter of support he had received from one of the
English Carmelite prioresses. He reiterated his willingness to cut short
his holiday and present the cardinal with a plan which would solve the
problem.

One section in Sternberg's telex may be seen to be of particular
significance:

> Since there is in Judaism no tradition of permanent contemplative
> prayer at any cemetery, we must reserve the right to ask that
> neither faith is permanently represented at the site which above
> all other places marks the graveyard of our people.

It was perhaps this appeal from the heart which prompted Macharski
to respond personally with a short telex dated 22 August, in which he
thanked Sternberg for his 'serious approach to my pronouncement'
and confessed that he made his decision 'with a heavy heart'. But
his position remained unchanged. Sternberg replied the same day,

expressing his 'deep disappointment and considerable concern' and took the cardinal to task for having 'chosen to see a demonstration by a small and totally unrepresentative group of individuals as typifying the response of Jews as a whole'.

In America, meanwhile, Tanenbaum was left to convey a non-partisan Jewish perpective on the 'religious wars'. In an op-ed in the *New York Post* of 18 August, he reiterated some of the contradictory arguments about the conflict that held him in thrall, including the contentious claims made years earlier by the Catholic fundraising group in Belgium envisaging the convent as a fortress guaranteeing 'the conversion of the strayed brothers from our countries'. Such statements have, indeed, been interpreted by various observers as confirmation that a prime aim of the Carmelites at Auschwitz was the posthumous conversion of its million Jewish dead. As Tanenbaum declared, these 'vague, mystical references ... resonated to many Jewish ears as a triumphal appeal to pursue the dead even beyond the grave'. He was equally critical of the huge cross, 'now the dominating religious symbol over Auschwitz'. 'Whether consciously intended or not,' he wrote, 'a revisionist scenario of history has been unfolding at the very gates of Auschwitz. Christians are being perceived as victims, not Jews.'

At the same time Tanenbaum hailed the perspicacity of Cardinal Albert Decourtray, one of the four cardinals who had signed the Geneva accords. He cited Decourtray's description of Auschwitz as the symbol of the attempt to totally exterminate the Jews and the cardinal's personal feeling that the construction of a convent in that place impinged on the dignity 'conferred on the Jewish people through its martyrs'. Tanenbaum firmly reiterated his belief that the commitments made by the Catholic negotiators at Geneva represented 'a major achievement in mutual comprehension' which 'must not be allowed to be side-tracked by provocative Jewish demonstrations or by violent Polish responses'.

Concluding his article in a more optimistic vein, Tanenbaum wrote that he had been told in Rome of a meeting between the Pope and the four cardinals in which the pontiff was reported to have said in Latin: 'An agreement entered into by the Church must be implemented.' That implementation, he envisaged, would be made possible "sooner rather than later" by 'patience and wisdom on the part of the authentic representatives of the Church and the mainstream Jewish community ... And Catholics and Jews will yet make another step forward in mutual comprehension'.

The Polish front, however, offered scant encouragement to such aspirations. One major casualty of the 'religious wars' was Cardinal Macharski's solidarity with the Jewish cause. He had, after all, been a signatory to the Geneva accords and had worked in co-operation with his Western Catholic counterparts and a high-level Jewish delegation. An indication of his concern for Jewish feelings about the convent at Auschwitz can be found in a letter to Cardinal Decourtray in early June which Decourtray cited in a letter to Théo Klein, leader of the Jewish delegation. It was clear that Macharski empathized with Jewish impatience and suffering; nevertheless, he was only too aware and would have wanted to warn his 'Jewish brothers' that any demonstrations and actions in front of the theatre building against the presence of the Carmelites would only prove counterproductive and reinforce Polish public opinion in its 'blind defence' of the nuns.

While deploring Macharski's volte-face as a 'serious violation' of the Geneva agreement, Tanenbaum felt obliged to attempt to assuage the ever-increasing hostility of Jewish opinion in America. He had spoken to Macharski's personal aide, Father Stanislav Musial, in Cracow and was impressed by Musial's friendly demeanour and by his assurances that the cardinal's statement did not constitute a 'break' or 'rupture' with the Jewish community. Reporting on this conversation in a Viewpoint article in the *Wisconsin Jewish Chronicle* of 25 August, he quoted Musial's interpretation of Macharski's infringement as a '"temporary interruption" provoked by the "invasion" of the convent by several self-appointed Jewish representatives from New York'. Tanenbaum went on to describe the Weiss incursion and how it 'violated Catholic feeling about the sanctity of their convents', most particularly in the case of the Carmelites, an order vowed to silence. He concluded by taking both sides to task:

> That insensitivity on both sides – far more serious on the part of the Polish violation of Auschwitz' meaning to Jews – must come to an end before we are locked into a cycle of 'reciprocal hostility.' We are now heavily engaged in trying to break that cycle on all sides.

The end of August was marked by two events in Poland of contrasting significance. On the political front, General Jaruzelski was replaced as prime minister by Tadeusz Mazowiecki, a Polish patriot and religious Christian who was deeply sympathetic to Jews and Judaism. The 'religious wars', on the other hand, gained momentum from the salvo fired by the Polish primate, Cardinal Glemp, whose long silence over the Auschwitz convent dispute can be seen, with hindsight, as ominous.

Glemp's homily on 26 August at the shrine of Czestochowa, in front of a congregation which included Prime Minister Mazowiecki, was to ensure that his name hit the headlines of the world's newspapers. Focusing on Polish–German and Polish–Jewish relations among other issues of the day, he appeared, initially, to be decrying stereotypes and certainly parts of his sermon contain appeals for peace and dialogue.

Nevertheless, his words were seized on, not without justification, as examples of classic anti-Semitic stereotyping. While conceding that there were 'Israelites' who gave their talents and their lives to Poland, he introduced 'Jew the innkeeper, who filled peasants with drink, and Jew the propagator of communism' as well as 'businessmen whose attitude to Poles was disrespectful and denigrating' and 'collaborators during the war who did not rise to the level of the heroic defenders of the Ghetto'.

In contrast to these negative depictions was a somewhat ambiguous statement that was equally unlikely to endear him to the Jewish world: 'Many Jews immersed themselves in Polish culture and in Christianity and the crosses on their graves do not nullify their love for their nation.' In view of the focus of the current controversy, this comment would appear quite insensitive. More offensive was his insinuation that Jews saw themselves as 'a nation elevated above all others' and his charge that Jews had the mass media at their disposal 'in many countries'.

But it was his interpretation of the Weiss fracas that was particularly sinister:

> Recently a squad of seven Jews from New York attacked the convent at Auschwitz and although this did not lead to the killing of the sisters or to the destruction of the convent because the attackers were restrained, they should not be regarded as heroes.

Not surprisingly Weiss, himself, used equally intemperate language, equating Glemp's statement to 'something out of the Middle Ages, a blood libel' and liable to incite a pogrom. Given the volatile mood in Poland as a result of the prolonged controversy over the Auschwitz convent, Weiss's reaction cannot be considered mere hyperbole.

The Czestochowa homily was severely criticized by the Solidarity newspaper *Gazeta Wyborcza* and failed to impress liberal Catholic opinion in Poland, which had long favoured the implementation of the Geneva accords. While winning himself support from more nationalistic circles at home which endorsed the outrage expressed by many inhabitants of Oswiecim (Auschwitz) at the decision to move the convent, Glemp's words enraged much of the Western world. Previously admired for his stance as a Polish patriot and courageous opponent of communism, the primate suddenly found doors closing on him. A projected trip to the United States, where previously he may well have been fêted as a hero, was cancelled for fear of violent protest.

Among the almost universal condemnation was Sternberg's relatively restrained telex of 29 August, in which he expressed himself 'greatly shocked' at Glemp's reported statement on Jews and Poland and asserted firmly that 'Jews have fought and died for Poland over the centuries and Poland was the scene of the greatest Jewish tragedy'. Sternberg concluded by assuming that Glemp was unaware of his earlier communications with Macharski and announced that he was sending copies of this telex to both Macharski and Mazowiecki.

For Tanenbaum, Glemp's behaviour 'added turmoil to the existing distress'. In a press release dated 3 September, he censured the Polish primate for betraying the 'letter and spirit' of the Second Vatican Council. 'It is evident there are two differing Catholic churches and two contrasting nationalisms in today's Poland,' he wrote. 'One is the old Polish church which was rigid, intolerant of other religions and deeply anti-Semitic. The newer church is constructed on the values and teachings of Vatican Council II and its commitment to positive Catholic–Jewish relations.' Condemning the old nationalism as 'authoritarian and oppressive', Tanenbaum took heart from the rise of the Solidarity movement, which offered a new nationalism that appeared tolerant and 'committed to democratric pluralism'. From his conversations with Polish leaders the previous week, Tanenbaum had learnt that Solidarity leaders were 'appalled' by Glemp's recent pronouncements. 'Cardinal Glemp may end up doing more damage to Poland's emerging new image and standing than the communists were even able to do,' he concluded.

5. September 1989:
Peace in Our Time?

There were signs that foreign reaction to the Glemp outburst was causing concern in Poland. On 6 September, Monseigneur Henryk Muszynski published a communiqué in favour of proceeding with the establishment of the centre proposed in the Geneva accords. This was sent to the Vatican. Two days later, the Polish Prime Minister wrote to Sternberg thanking him for the good wishes he had sent him in his capacity of convenor of the Religious Press Group. Mazowiecki declared himself 'deeply moved' by prayers for Poland and the Polish people said in synagogues in Britain and the United States, which he wished to reciprocate, and issued an open invitation to Sternberg to visit Poland and meet with him. Significantly, his letter spoke of 'the untold suffering of the Jewish people whose each and every member stands unequaled [sic] among all martirized [sic] nations' and of 'the tragedy and sacrifice of *shoah*', which 'defies any comparison'. These words were in contrast to Glemp's Czestochowa sermon which described 'Jews, Poles, Gypsies' as common victims of 'Hitler's strategy of extermination'.

By the middle of the third week of September, events were moving quickly. To compensate for the cancelled trip to America, Glemp decided to come to England. At the same time, the Vatican announced, through Cardinal Willebrands of the Commission for Religious Relations with Judaism, that it endorsed Monseigneur Muszynski's communiqué regarding the intention to proceed with the establishment of the much-discussed Centre for Information, Meeting, Dialogue and Prayer outside Auschwitz. The Holy See was convinced that such a centre would contribute significantly to relations between Christians and Jews and that the proposed new convent 'at the heart of this centre' would play a decisive part in its success.

On releasing the announcement to the press on 19 September, the Vatican broke its silence on the contentious issue that had strained Catholic–Jewish relations for so long. No less significant was its decision to offer financial assistance to 'this important but costly project'.

An Associated Press correspondent reported an immediate response from Jewish leaders in the United States who 'applauded the statement'. Cardinal Glemp, however, in Bristol for the consecration of a Polish Catholic church the same day, was unaware of the Vatican announcement.

In London, Sternberg was busy polishing his Polish credentials. The day before Glemp's Bristol visit, he was at the Polish embassy with the deputy director general of the Institute of Directors discussing the possibility of setting up joint ventures with Polish businesses, a subject close to the Polish ambassador's heart. Sternberg had come armed with Prime Minister Mazowiecki's letter inviting him to Poland and suggested leading a delegation of British business leaders there. At the same time he was mooting a strategy to take advantage of Glemp's presence in England.

Sternberg and Glemp had already rubbed shoulders at a meeting of the St Egidio, a group of forward-looking lay and religious Catholics who had important contacts with members of other faiths. Not surprisingly, then, the Cardinal was keen to meet with this Jewish Papal Knight, despite the less than enthusiastic letter he had received from Sternberg a few weeks earlier. Sternberg, however, had his own agenda:

> Glemp wanted to meet me at the airport and I wasn't going to meet him at the airport. I told the Polish ambassador that it was no good my meeting him. He must sign a letter that he was going to remove the convent. That was the only way I was going to meet him.

In the event a dinner meeting was arranged at the Polish ambassador's spacious residence in Templewood Avenue, Hampstead, north London, for the evening of 20 September. Sternberg was due to come accompanied by the Chief Rabbi, Lord Jakobovits, and Dr Lionel Kopelovitz, the President of the Board of Deputies. But a press conference Glemp gave in Bristol the day before put paid to their attendance.

At the press conference Glemp, while paying lip service, as ever, to the need for dialogue, was in a less than conciliatory mood. After formulating a critique of what he called Jewish '*Shoah* theology' which was none too sympathetic, he made vague noises of support for the prayer centre outside Auschwitz. While he hinted that the nuns might eventually consider moving there, he made it clear that they would receive his backing even if they refused to do so. The Geneva accords were dismissed as 'wishful thinking'. When the cardinal was eventually informed of the Vatican's newly released announcement, his reaction was decidedly cool.

Glemp's clumsy handling of these sensitive issues was to prove his

Achilles' heel. Initially, however, it was Sternberg who was put on the spot:

> I was in great trouble because I promised him that he was going to meet the Chief Rabbi and the President of the Board of Deputies. Now, somebody else would have told him, 'I'm sorry, I cannot bring you the Chief Rabbi and I cannot bring you the President of the Board of Deputies either, so therefore you must meet me on my own.' Of course, that's not the way to operate.

Sternberg was also under pressure not to attend himself. Jakobovits and Kopelovitz had advised him against it: 'Please don't meet him because this man will only humiliate you and you won't get anywhere with him.'

In the event Sternberg took Rabbi Tony Bayfield, Director of the Sternberg Centre for Judaism, and Professor Antony Polonsky, an expert on Polish affairs at the London School of Economics. Glemp came accompanied by 'a galaxy of priests' and they were all sitting down in the dining room of the ambassador's residence.

Underneath the façade of pleasantries, Sternberg was very annoyed. 'I was in a corner in so far as no one wanted to come with me except Bayfield and Polonsky and when you're in a corner you act accordingly, then you fight.' This was something he had learnt in his business dealings. 'I'm a very peaceful person, I never start a row with anyone, except if someone puts me in a corner.'

It was Glemp's turn to face Sternberg's well-honed negotiating tactics. Little was he to know that the paranoia he expressed at Czestochowa about Jews controlling the media was to be used against him:

> Glemp said Jews are very powerful people. When people say that, I say yes, the Jews are very powerful people, we're very clever and we're very powerful and we rule the world. Why should I have disabused him?

On a practical level, Sternberg intended to telephone Clifford Longley, then Religious Affairs Editor at *The Times*, if things moved his way. He was perfectly aware that the beleagured cardinal might be vulnerable to such a display of 'media manipulation'. But he was none too confident himself. 'I was very concerned that this man was not going to sign anything. That was my greatest worry because I was told he was not going to sign anything and if he doesn't sign anything, then I look like a monkey.'

Sternberg had rarely felt so exposed. His reputation was in danger of being mauled by recalcitrance on the part of the cardinal. In a fax he had sent the Polish ambassador that morning, explaining that Jakobovits and Kopelovitz would not be attending the dinner, he had been quite candid. Unless the cardinal signed a letter and press statement he had had prepared, he, Sternberg, would lose all credibility with world Jewry. 'The Cardinal will have demolished the only link existing between world Jewry and the Vatican,' he wrote, equally concerned that failure would damage the work in which he took such pride.

Knowing that he was taking 'a huge risk' in meeting Glemp in these circumstances, Sternberg was as disarming as possible. With the greatest courtesy he explained to the cardinal, 'You've put me in a very difficult situation coming and seeing you here'. But he sensed, at the same time, that he could do Glemp a favour. 'You must always give someone a figleaf, to climb down, it's very important,' he explains. And the figleaf he was offering Glemp was the chance to repudiate what he had said in Bristol. 'You can say you have been misunderstood, misquoted and misunderstood. I want to ring *The Times* and you'll have a very nice leader in *The Times*.'

There are conflicting accounts of how long it took before Glemp actually signed. Clifford Longley remembers that he received a phone call at 9pm, just in time to change the unfavourable leader about Glemp he had prepared for the first edition of *The Times*. Many reports at the time gave the impression that Glemp, having found a sympathetic Jew who would listen to him, poured out his heart for several hours – and then he signed. Sternberg insists today that the heart-to-heart was after the signing:

> He signed first because I told him, 'We know exactly why we are here. You've got to sign this letter, it's very important this letter.' And then I phoned *The Times* and then he signed the letter and later he said he didn't realize that there are such nice people, that Jews are such nice, understanding people.

In the famous letter, theoretically in response to Sternberg's telex to him, Glemp affirmed his intention of implementing the Geneva accords of 1987. He cited both the sympathetic awareness of Jewish suffering in Prime Minister Mazowiecki's letter to Sternberg, which he claimed to have seen, and the Pope's reference to the 'immense suffering of the Jews in Poland' and welcomed the opportunity to meet Sternberg in Poland. He was glad, too, to learn that 'some of the shrill voices do not reflect the feelings of world Jewry and aggression is not part of Jewish philosophy'. As Longley's leader in the second edition of *The Times* put it: 'Cardinal Glemp ... unexpectedly accepted an olive branch offered to him at the last minute by a group of British Jewish leaders, and responded generously.'

Congratulations were now the order of the day. One of the first of many dignitaries to express gratification for the new beginning was Lord Jakobovits who, in a letter to Glemp, praised the cardinal for helping 'to do much to restore the mutual respect between our two great faiths, building on the goodwill and understanding initiated by the late lamented Pope John XXIII'.

Not content to rest on his laurels, Sternberg and his wife made a quick trip to Rome with Bishop Gerald Mahon, Vice-Chairman of the British Council of Christians and Jews, hoping to consolidate the progress which had been achieved. He met twice with Father Sainz de Baranda, the Carmelite Superior General, and his English-speaking spokesman, Father Anthony Morello. At the Vatican he engaged in discussions with Cardinals Willebrands and Casaroli.

While Sainz de Baranda expressed satisfaction that a solution of 'the problem' had been reached, Sternberg asked for a formal declaration that the Carmelite Order would support the Geneva accords. This the Superior General 'found an easy request to oblige'. Through Father Morello he made the following declaration:

> Since we are dealing not with suppression but rather the transferral of a monastery, we will be happy to see our Carmelite Nuns relocated once there is provided for them a permanent monastery within the complex of the Auschwitz Centre of Prayer and Information foreseen by the Geneva Declaration.

A statement released by Father Morello at the end of Sternberg's visit spoke of the 'good rapport' established between Sternberg and the Generalate (the Superior General's headquarters).

On his return to London, Sternberg, too, was flooded with messages acclaiming his 'constructive role' in resolving the conflict and thanked by more than one signatory of the Geneva accords for his 'relentless efforts to improve the dialogue between Jews and Christians'. Not least was a cordial telex dated 29 September from Cardinal Glemp himself, expressing his appreciation of Sternberg's 'opennes [sic] to solve a difficult problems [sic] and the understanding of others'. Glemp also welcomed the invitation Sternberg had extended to visit the Sternberg Centre and indeed did do so at a later date.

How widely the events of 20 September were reported in Europe is another matter. The Polish left-wing daily *Trybuna Ludu* of 23–24 September did indeed have an account and quoted Sternberg, described as an 'eminent Jewish spokesman', as being 'delighted' with the positive development: 'Cardinal Glemp has seen that we Jews are sensible people and this is a victory for common sense.' On the other hand, in a letter of 2 October faxed to Tanenbaum, Sternberg refers to the Munich daily *Süddeutsche Zeitung*, cited in the *Herald Tribune* and comments: 'I have heard that it is not we who solved the problem but it was solved by other methods. This lie will have to be countered.'

How Tanenbaum reacted to Sternberg's missive is a matter for conjecture. A few days earlier, on 29 September, he had released a commentary article via the Jewish Telegraphic Agency (JTA) which hailed the recent Vatican declaration 'calling publicly and officially' for the convent's removal as 'a turning point in the five year controversy'. Tanenbaum was particularly encouraged that the Vatican had committed itself to contributing financially to the building of a new convent in the proposed interfaith centre and that several Catholic churches in Europe had indicated that they would also contribute. 'To use a colloquial expression, when you put your money where your mouth is, that's serious,' he wrote. On the other hand, he was strongly opposed to the idea that Jews should finance the new building and was particularly concerned by a report that Zygmund Nissenbaum, a Polish Jew from Germany, had offered to pay for the new convent:

> Were that to take place, the Polish anti-Semites and others will not only propagandize that Jews 'own' the media and the banks, but that they are now buying out the Catholic Church. Besides, it is morally offensive to think that Jews have to buy back Auschwitz.

Tanenbaum had also received a letter from the newly elected Polish prime minister and was moved by Mazowiecki's 'remarkable, sympathetic understanding of the uniqueness of the Shoah to the Jewish people'. He was optimistic that 'between this Vatican move and the Polish government's efforts to resolve the convent issue,' a new situation was unfolding.

Tanenbaum had been looking forward to accompanying Sternberg to Poland at the invitation of Mazowiecki, Glemp and Macharski. Ever the thoughtful visionary, he was aware of a 'major intellectual, religious/cultural and political struggle' going on in that country and was convinced that Poland needed 'serious Jewish attention'. In another commentary article released via the JTA on October 27, he referred to the period before the Second World War when the old political culture in Poland and the traditional Catholic Church 'reinforced each other by using anti-Semitism to assert their domination over the Polish people'. Now, however, there was a new Poland being formed under Mazowiecki and the then Solidarity leader, Lech Walesa, 'who are ashamed of that hateful past and who wish to forge a new relationship with world Jewry and Israel'. 'It is in the interests of the democratic West, and especially of Israel and world Jewry, to have a Poland reasonably free of its chronic anti-Jewish past', he wrote.

The purpose of the proposed visit to Poland, as Tanenbaum informed his readers, was not only to assist in hastening the building of a new convent away from Auschwitz; it was also to 'help establish programs in key areas of Polish culture and religion that will in time uproot the worst weeds of anti-Semitism'. In the event ill health and the freezing temperatures of the Polish winter prevented Tanenbaum from taking part in the long-planned mission.

The proposed trip to Poland was also the subject of a letter to Sternberg from Théo Klein, leader of the Jewish delegation at Geneva, who was eager that the Geneva negotiators should remain involved in steps taken towards resolving the conflict. In his reply, Sternberg outlined the various aims of his visit, one of which was to encourage the establishment of a Council of Christians and Jews in Poland.

Sternberg did indeed visit Poland at the end of November, and succeeded in relaunching the Rotary Club in Warsaw, another of his aims. Together with Professor Polonsky, who had accompanied him to the crucial dinner in September, he also called on Cardinal Glemp. By this time Glemp was telling them, together with a delegation of the American Jewish Congress, of his wish to concentrate his efforts on the promotion of Catholic–Jewish understanding, particularly at the popular level, where 'ignorance of Jews and Judaism is widespread'.

6. 1989–91:
One Step Forward, Another Step Back

Despite the apparent success of the efforts of Sternberg and his associates and the Vatican's ostensible interest in seeing the conflict satisfactorily resolved, a considerable degree of scepticism prevailed among
influential voices within American Jewry. It was perhaps inevitable
that, for many Jews, the current controversy evoked memories of the
Vatican's silence during the Holocaust.

No more encouraging was an interview given by Sister Teresa, the
Mother Superior of the Carmelites at Auschwitz, to *The Post Eagle*, a
Polish American weekly that supported the presence of the nuns at
the site of the former concentration camp. The defiant message with
which she ended her interview: – 'You can tell the Americans that we
are not moving an inch' – was hardly calculated to reassure American
Jews any more than the unsavoury blend of anti-Semitism and ignorance
with which the interview was liberally sprinkled.

This scepticism was something with which Tanenbaum felt obliged
to contend. He was aware, however, of evidence emerging of a range
of activities that had been taking place between Poles and Jews for
several years in the academic, intellectual and religious spheres and
it was this that he brought to the attention of American–Jewish readers
in another commentary article released by the JTA on 22 December.
He supported his claim that Poland had suddenly become 'the most
active arena for Christian–Jewish relations' with a report on Sternberg
and Polonsky's mission to Poland the previous month, which he had
been unable to join.

Despite the upbeat tone of much of the article, Tanenbaum's objective was, of course, not merely to present a rosy picture of Christian–
Jewish relations in Poland. He knew that the protracted conflict over
the convent had been instrumental in fuelling anti-Semitism in Poland
and needed to make every effort to prevent Jewish opinion in America
from erupting once again as was likely if the facts on the ground failed
to match expectations. Consequently his article concluded with a clear
warning:

Polish Jews are now deeply worried that 'irresponsible actions or statements by Jews abroad, with little knowledge of Polish conditions, enormously complicate conditions'. They pleaded with us 'to use your influence to persuade Western Jews to refrain from provocative statements or actions'.

Sternberg, for his part, was continuing to press for temporary accommodation for the nuns to be erected as soon as possible, fearing, justifiably, that Christian–Jewish relations would once again be jeopardized if building work were held up. Already at the turn of the year, the impatience of many in the Jewish world found expression in a full-page advertisement placed by some organizations in Israel in the *Jerusalem Post*'s international edition. The advertisement, signed by the chief rabbis of Israel, mayors, other rabbis and various personalities, announced a campaign to collect support and signatures against the delay in the implementation of the Geneva accords. At the same time Rabbi Avi Weiss was intent on pursuing a libel suit against Cardinal Glemp, for which he had engaged Alan Dershowitz, a well-known American trial lawyer.

In an attempt to quell these latest rumblings which were liable to disturb the delicate new *status quo*, Sternberg took to the press, in the *International Herald Tribune* and the London *Times*, to urge patience, restraint and understanding, now that the accords had the backing of the Polish primate and the Vatican. The new year had seen Cardinal Edward Cassidy replace Cardinal Willebrands as head of the Vatican's Commission for Religious Relations with Judaism. Cassidy was fully behind the implementation of the accords. However, in a letter to the *Herald Tribune* published on 31 January, Isi Liebler, a vice-president of the WJC based in Melbourne, took issue with Sternberg's stance which, he claimed, reflected 'insensitivity to Jewish concerns', particularly as 'not one spade has been put in the ground' to symbolize the convent's removal.

Building work on the new centre did eventually start on 19 February 1990 when, as reported in some Western newspapers, 'a Roman Catholic cardinal and a Polish government minister dug the first spadefuls of earth to build the interfaith centre'. The cardinal in question was Macharski, who rose to the occasion with moving oratory: 'May justice, peace and love radiate from this place. May people draw the strength here to overcome everything that divides them.' This tangible demonstration of good faith was reciprocated on 27 February, when Moshe Arens, Israel's foreign minister, signed an agreement in Warsaw resuming diplomatic relations between the two countries which had been severed at the time of the Six Day War in 1967.

The symbolic 'launch' of construction work might also have bought some months of quiet while the world waited for the building to be ready. By the autumn, with no progress reports forthcoming, Sternberg took the opportunity of responding to a letter from Glemp to ask the cardinal when he anticipated the completion of the centre. As a sweetener, he suggested that a colloquium could be arranged to mark the inauguration.

Despite the absence of any breakthrough on the building front, 1991 brought a notable advance in the attitude of the Polish Church towards the Jewish people. On Sunday, 20 January a letter from the Polish bishops on the relationship of Christians to Jews and Judaism was read in all churches in Poland. Written to mark the twenty-fifth anniversary of the Vatican II document *Nostra Aetate*, the letter contained an unambiguous statement of regret for 'all incidents of anti-Semitism which were committed by anyone on Polish soil' and expressed sorrow for 'all injustices and harm done to Jews'.

In ironic contrast were the tactics used by the Solidarity leader and national hero, Lech Walesa, in launching his campaign to become president in the autumn of 1990. Walesa played on Poland's deep-rooted tradition of anti-Semitism to discredit his principal rival, Tadeusz Masowiecki, whom he himself had named as the country's first non-communist prime minister. Mazowiecki was accused of being a secret Jew because of his pro-Jewish sympathies. Much was made of the assertion that people should 'declare their origins', giving rise, among anti-Semites, to the phobia of excessive Jewish influence in government. The word 'Jew', moreover, was used to denote a person who got rich at someone else's expense. Walesa himself declared that he was 'a full-blooded Pole with documents going back to his ancestors to prove it'.

Reactions in the West to these fresh demonstrations of what Adam Michnik, a leading Polish dissident of Jewish origin, described as 'wounding anti-Semitic rhetoric', were none too favourable, particularly as the situation was highlighted in a television documentary series about the new Polish president. In the event Walesa, who was hardly an anti-Semite at heart, placated observers in the West by moving swiftly to mend fences with the Jewish world. He created a Council on Polish–Jewish Relations with a brief to fight anti-Semitism and improve relations with Jews; at the same time a measure was put forward in the Polish parliament to preserve historic synagogues and other Jewish landmarks. Walesa himself received a number of Western Jewish leaders after being elected president and discussed Jewish matters in interviews with Reuters and the popular Israeli newspaper *Yediot Acharonot*.

Walesa's trip to the United States in March 1991 was marked by a conspicuous number of high-profile activities with a Jewish orientation, including a speech in Washington at the site of the Holocaust Memorial Museum then in construction. Admitting that he had made mistakes, he used these occasions to distance himself from some of his indiscretions at the time of the election campaign. On his visit to Israel in May, Walesa went even further in his speech to the Knesset, the Israeli parliament, when he asked the Jewish people for 'forgiveness' for Polish behaviour during the Second World War.

More challenging for the Polish president was a meeting with the World Federation of Polish Jews at the Diaspora Museum near Tel Aviv. Discarding his prepared speech after listening to a stream of complaints about the resurgence of anti-Semitism in Poland and other matters, Walesa won his audience round with a spontaneous, emotionally uplifting response. As the *Jerusalem Post* reported: 'The ambivalence and open hostility which had initially permeated the atmosphere of the auditorium gradually dissipated as he talked.' Commentators have observed, however, that the Polish president's fulsome denunciations of anti-Semitism on his travels were intended in the main for Western consumption and had little impact on dampening anti-Semitism in his own country, where his popularity was waning.

A more positive development within Poland was the establishment at Sternberg's initiative of a Christian–Jewish Dialogue Division within the Polish–Israeli Friendship Society. Chaired by Stanislav Krajewski and Waldemar Chrostowski, both of whom had been involved in the dispute over the convent at Auschwitz, the Dialogue Division won the support of the chief rabbi of Poland and of Monseigneur Muszynski, whose Commission for Dialogue with Judaism had recently held a theological symposium in Cracow under the auspices of the International Council of Christians and Jews. Both Krajewski and Chrostowski, moreover, were members of Walesa's Council on Polish–Jewish Relations. While both were aware of the hard work needed in attempting to reconcile Poles and Jews, Krajewski was wary that the Council might be used to promote the president's credibility in the West.

Another seed of goodwill was sown in June when Pope John Paul II made his fourth visit to his homeland and met five members of Poland's Jewish community. In what might be seen as a foreshadowing of the Vatican's recognition of Israel, which would only be consummated some two and a half years later, he told them that the creation of the state of Israel was 'an act of historical justice'.

Despite this upswing in Polish–Jewish activities, there was little progress in the building of the new centre where the convent was to be relocated. Already in March Sternberg had received a letter from Father Marek Glownia, President of the Board of the Cracow Foundation, who was responsible for overseeing the construction work and administration of the centre. At the outset of what was to develop into a lengthy correspondence, Glownia had explained the difficulties of building during the winter months and had indicated that there were also financial problems. In his reply, Sternberg expressed optimism that the joint efforts of the Polish government and the Catholic Church would facilitate the completion of the venture.

Less optimistic was a report from Serge Cwajgenbaum, Secretary General of the European Jewish Congress, following a journey to Poland in June. Cwajgenbaum had visited the site of the convent at Auschwitz and was shocked to observe that the sisters were continuing to build and that a new wing had been added to the existing building. At the site of the proposed new centre, he was given to understand that while the first of five planned buildings had been partly constructed, it would be at least two or three years before the centre was completed.

On receiving Cwajgenbaum's report, Hayim Pinner, Director of the Sternberg Charitable Foundation, conveyed his concern to the Polish authorities but received no explanation about the extension to the convent. Although an elegant leaflet advertising the prospective centre with a discreet request for funding was published in August 1991 with messages from Cardinal Macharski and Pope John Paul II himself, it was clear there was going to be no opening in the foreseeable future.

In the meantime, Father Camilo Maccise, newly elected as Superior General of the Carmelite order in Rome, had made clear in a letter in July to Théo Klein, one of the Geneva signatories, that he, personally, was determined to see the Geneva accords implemented as soon as possible. 'I express to you my regrets for the lack of understanding and respect due to the Jewish memory that may have been demonstrated by members of the Carmelite family,' the new Superior General wrote. However, having weighed up the current situation, he felt it impractical to envisage a transfer of the Carmelite sisters to the new convent before October the following year.

The depth of the Superior General's evident understanding and empathy with Jewish feelings evoked a warm response from Klein. As a rejoinder to Maccise's reassurance that the Carmelite sisters were at one with his wishes, Klein assured him that the Jewish negotiators had nothing against the sisters. 'We wish that they may fulfil their vocation in the new convent which is under construction.' Significantly, Klein also made clear that it was hoped that the cross, 'put down in defiance to our agreement', would be moved to stand in front of the new convent.

Other Jewish leaders in the Francophone countries welcomed the new Carmelite Superior General's heartfelt goodwill but were sceptical as to the results this was likely to produce. In an article in *Le Monde* of

10 August entitled 'To Avoid the Christianisation of Auschwitz', the President of CRIF, Jean Kahn, voiced the unease experienced by many Jews over the fact that such heavy weather was being made of transferring some ten Carmelite sisters to new accommodation only hundreds of metres from the camp's perimeter six years after the first Geneva declaration in 1986.

Even after the move, Kahn pointed out, the proximity of the new convent, reinforced by the cross near the present building, would ensure that Auschwitz would continue to be a focal point of 'spiritual tourism' for numerous pilgrims for whom the Christianization of Auschwitz was already a *fait accompli*. A particularly disturbing factor, as Kahn saw it, was the subliminal desire of the pilgrims and the Carmelites to convert not only the living but the dead – 'who would thus see themselves murdered a second time'.

Kahn's words were endorsed by the President of the Belgian Committee of Jewish Organisations, Lazard Perez, who proposed that the European Jewish Congress should meet to take a stand on the current situation. Perez had opposed the 'softly softly' policy which had prevailed between 1987 and 1989 after the second Geneva meeting and was not disposed to repeat the procedure in anticipation of the projected transfer of the Carmelites in October 1992. Writing in the Belgian newspaper *Le Soir* on 27 August, he took issue with the latest delay in implementing the Geneva accords: 'These successive delays themselves generate further delays due to the numerous obstacles that come to light in the meantime.'

Perez highlighted the incongruity which enabled generous provision to be found for the expansion and improvement of the Carmelites' present, supposedly makeshift, abode in the old theatre building while financial constraints were cited as reasons for the delay in constructing the new centre. In order to prevent a further deterioration in the current interfaith climate he proposed that the Carmelites should be offered temprorary alternative accommodation straightaway.

7. Autumn 1991:
Was the Cardinal a *Ba'al Teshuvah*?

Not surprisingly, the lack of progress in effecting the transfer of the Carmelites at Auschwitz ensured that tensions within the American Jewish community were running high at the prospect of Cardinal Glemp's arrival in September. Rabbi Avi Weiss had announced that he would have the cardinal served with legal papers charging him with slander, libel and defamation. Kalman Sultanik, a Vice President of the World Jewish Congress, urged Glemp to apologize or to cancel his visit, claiming it would be an insult and a provocation to American Jews.

For Rabbi Marc Tanenbaum, who had been struggling with ill health for several months, Glemp's visit, at the invitation of the US Conference of Catholic Bishops, posed a special challenge. Tanenbaum knew very well that an excessively hostile response from Jewish leaders might do untold damage to the fragile edifice of Polish–Jewish understanding that was emerging in the post-communist era. In his notes for a column to be released by the Jewish Telegraphic Agency at the end of August, he warned against allowing 'some self-appointed individuals to snatch defeat from victory', although he toned down his rhetoric in the final published version.

Tanenbaum's task was made easier by a move by the cardinal, himself, a few days earlier. Mindful, no doubt, of the Weiss slander action, Glemp had made public a letter he had written to Archbishop Adam Maida of Detroit expressing regret for having implied in his infamous Czestochowa homily of 1989 that the 'seven Jewish demonstrators' who had scaled the walls of the convent at Auschwitz intended physical harm to the Carmelites or the destruction of their convent. In the same letter he had branded anti-Semitism an evil 'contrary to the spirit of the Gospel'.

Defending the cardinal in his JTA column, Tanenbaum took advantage of the imminence of the Jewish high holy days to examine Glemp's conduct in the context of *teshuvah* or repentance. After giving a few details of the cardinal's humble background and his lack of schooling during the Nazi occupation of Poland, he acknowledged the offensiveness of the Czestochowa sermon but pointed out that it had

drawn strong protests from Catholic leaders as well as Jews. Tanenbaum
then listed three instances in which the cardinal had appeared to take
a changed stance: his letter of 20 September 1989 acknowledging
Jewish suffering in the *Shoah* and committing himself to the 1987 Geneva
declaration; the authority he had given, as primate, to the declaration
of the Polish Catholic hierarchy condemning anti-Semitism which was
read out in every Catholic church in Poland on 20 January that year;
and his regrets over the implications of the Czestochowa homily.

'I do not know whether Cardinal Glemp is a genuine *ba'al teshuvah*,'
Tanenbaum wrote. 'But he and the Polish Catholic church he leads
have shown demonstrable signs that they are undergoing serious
corrective changes in their attitudes towards Jews, Judaism, the Nazi
Holocaust and Israel.'

Glemp's intentions were to be put to the test at a meeting in Washington with a delegation from the International Jewish Committee for Inter-
religious Consultations, of which Tanenbaum was a prominent member.
Who, on the Jewish side, was actually going to meet with the cardinal
was the burning question which divided American Jewish leaders. Frus-
trated by the inability to reach a consensus, the head of IJCIC, Seymour
Reich, resigned his post a few days before the scheduled meeting.

A dozen representatives from six Jewish organizations were expected
to attend the meeting. Some had expressed reservations as to whether
Cardinal Glemp had addressed various other controversial aspects of
his Czestochowa sermon but appreciated that no benefit could come
from refusing to meet him. Two or three others, including Abraham
Foxman, director of the Anti-Defamation League of B'nai Brith,
demanded that the cardinal repudiate specific statements he had
made including the inference that Jews held the mass media at their
disposal in many countries.

These contradictory responses were the subject of an article
Tanenbaum wrote for the *Baltimore Jewish Times* a week before the
cardinal's arrival. He urged American Jewish leaders to keep in mind
the crude anti-Semitic themes expressed at Czestochowa but also
to acknowledge the important changes that had taken place since
1989 and build on them to strengthen the movement towards uprooting anti-Semitism in Poland. At the same time he warned that if Glemp
were humiliated on his arrival in Boston by having a sentence served
on him – an action that would 'gratify the egos of two or three individuals' – the consequences could be 'exceedingly damaging' not only
to 'the pitiful Polish Jewish remnant' but also to American Jewry itself.

It was a troubling time for American Jewry with the Bush administration locked in confrontation with the Shamir government over the
Israelis' demand for $10 billion in loan guarantees, a conflict which,

Tanenbaum cautioned, could give rise to significant negative fallout. Equally disquieting were the recent riots in the Crown Heights district of Brooklyn which had thrown the spotlight on a pervasive culture of vicious anti-Semitism among many black Americans. Any public explosion against Cardinal Glemp would add fuel to the flames and run the risk of alienating the entire American Catholic hierarchy and numerous Polish Catholics in the United States. To drive his point home, Tanenbaum took to task those Jewish leaders who felt justified in provoking further animosity towards Jews, ignoring the fact that they were elected to office to defend Jewish interests and assure Jewish security.

At times like this, Tanenbaum may have felt that his was a voice in the wilderness. Glemp's arrival in Washington for the meeting with Jewish leaders on Friday, 20 September was greeted by demonstrators picketing the headquarters of the National Conference of Catholic Bishops where the meeting was to be held. The protesters were chanting Hebrew dirges and carrying placards demanding an apology.

But what exactly constitutes an apology? Ultimately it was this somewhat nebulous definition that lay at the heart of the controversy. At the meeting, boycotted in the last resort by officials of four major Jewish organizations because the cardinal refused to apologize, Glemp once again expressed regret for his remarks at Czestochowa which, he said, were based on mistaken information. However, since he appeared to be unwilling to retract his remarks and make a formal apology, Alan Dershowitz issued a libel writ against him on behalf of Rabbi Avi Weiss. The cardinal was left to prepare to defend himself in court.

Many of the 12 Jewish leaders who did attend the meeting said that their absent colleagues were looking for too literal an apology. As Tanenbaum made clear in a statement to the *International Herald Tribune*: 'Cardinals never apologize, not to Catholics and certainly not to us. He knows he made a grievous error; that was his way of saying it.' Glemp's commitment to work with the Jewish leaders 'to combat anti-Semitism at its very roots' enabled the majority of the Jewish contingent to come away encouraged.

More significant, perhaps, was the effect of the meeting on Glemp, himself, as Tanenbaum reported in *The Jewish Week*. Describing the meeting as a 'fundamental encounter' and citing one of his rabbinical colleagues who commented that 'there was an exchange and there was change', Tanenbaum expressed confidence that the cardinal could be educated, or re-educated, about Jews and Judaism.

It appeared that Glemp had never met such a large group of Jewish people. It was evident, too, that his ignorance of the elementary facts about Jewish history, religion and culture in his country had made him susceptible to absorbing the most primitive and vicious stereotypes of

Polish folklore. To educate the cardinal, some of the more scholarly
rabbis present at the meeting reviewed both 'the grandeur and the
misery' of Jewish existence in Poland since the thirteenth century. The
cardinal was then told that Jews had the right to expect the head of
the Polish church 'not to bear false witness'.

The cardinal emerged 'determined to change' and explained that the
pastoral letter of January 1991 'was written in the spirit of repentance,
teshuvah, on the part of Polish Catholics'. The Jewish delegation 'felt
it was both wise and responsible to receive his "teshuvah" as such and
not seek foolishly to compel the cardinal to grovel'.

A positive follow-up to the Washington meeting was Glemp's statement in Boston expressing appreciation for the talks and pledging a
continuation of the dialogue in Warsaw the following year. Archbishop
William Keeler of Baltimore, the key figure in Catholic–Jewish relations
on the National Conference of Catholic Bishops, was left to organize
the proposed meeting together with his Polish counterpart, Bishop
Henryk Muszynski.

The first steps towards the proposed dialogue were taken at a further
meeting in New York on 6 October between the Polish primate and
Jewish leaders. This meeting, hosted by Cardinal John O'Connor, was
also picketed by hosts of chanting, banner-waving Jewish protesters.
In the face of this, O'Connor pointed out to his Polish guest that the
presence of the Jewish leaders who had come to meet him demanded
no small measure of courage.

The apparent success of the Washington and New York meetings
was marked by Sternberg with a press release from London in which
he expressed disappointment with those American Jewish leaders who
had refused to meet the Polish primate. At the same time he 'noted
with satisfaction' that the cardinal was carrying out the understanding
reached between them as contained in the letter signed by Glemp two
years earlier on 20 September 1989.

But as Gerhart Riegner of the WJC once observed, Christian–Jewish
relations are like a glass that may be perceived as half-full or half-
empty. A far less upbeat perspective on prospects for the removal of
the Auschwitz convent and on the Polish primate's intentions emerged
during a meeting in October 1991 between representatives of the
Board of Deputies of British Jews, including its president, Israel
Finestein, and the Polish ambassador, Tadeusz de Virion, whose father
was a leading Polish General who was also murdered at Auschwitz.
The meeting, arranged by the Board, was 'to discuss various issues of
concern to the Jewish community'.

The Jewish delegates were unhappy with the lack of progress on the
new building work outside Auschwitz and noted with concern that exten-

sions had been made to the existing convent. They were also disturbed by reports suggesting that some camp buildings were being used for commercial purposes. While assuring them that the Carmelites would definitely be moving out of their existing building, the ambassador could not specify when, 'as money was short'. He appeared surprised, nevertheless, that the move was taking so long.

Cardinal Glemp also came in for criticism. The Jewish delegates drew attention to 'recent remarks' the Polish primate had made suggesting that Jews had been responsible for Poland's economic problems before the war and that they had also been involved in pushing alchohol to the Polish people. Since the primate had enormous influence, his remarks were often reflected in the sermons of parish priests. Once again the ambassador was duly sympathetic and agreed that the cardinal's remarks 'appeared to be foolish'. In order to pursue the matter, however, he would need to know the precise words the cardinal had used.

It is intriguing to speculate on the genesis of the 'recent remarks' in view of the fact that the meeting took place on 24 October and *The Tablet* of 19 October reported on Cardinal Glemp's relatively positive appraisal of his American visit after his return to Warsaw. The cardinal, it appeared, had found a 'distinct desire for dialogue' among leaders of American Jewry and believed that the dialogue, although difficult, 'had been carried out in truth'. While he had declined to discuss the protests of Weiss and his adherents, he did disclose that these had had no negative effect on the dialogue.

Since the Polish primate did not feature in the news columns of the following week's edition of *The Tablet*, it might be suggested that the Jewish delegation were basing their criticism on remarks made at Czestochowa two years earlier and recycled in the press at the time of Glemp's visit to America. It would appear, then, that for activists in Christian–Jewish dialogue like Sternberg and Tanenbaum the Polish horizon may have looked rosy with promise, while to Jews uninvolved in dialogue it remained overcast.

One significant topic was brought up in the course of the 24 October meeting which foreshadowed later controversies. This was the Polish ambassador's suggestion that an international, inter-religious memorial on the site of the Auschwitz death camp would be the best way to solve the disputes between the opposing faiths. This suggestion did not find favour with the delegation from the Board, however. Finestein, the president, opposed any denominational or inter-denominational facilities at Auschwitz. In his view, the best response would be to provide an opportunity for meditation in total silence. It will be seen that this perspective, held by a number of prominent Jews, did not resonate with many Poles, who continued to visit Auschwitz in the coming years.

8. Early 1992:
Stumbling Forward

The year 1991 ended with 'October 1992' trotted out like a magic formula to answer any query or assuage any anxiety about the eventual opening of the new convent and centre. In late November the cornerstone of the new convent was laid by Cardinal Macharski. The cornerstone had been specially blessed by Pope John Paul II and was brought from Rome for the ceremony by Cardinal Cassidy.

Earlier in November, however, the European Jewish Congress had convened in Berlin and anticipated that promises relating to the Carmelites moving by the end of 1992 would not be fulfilled. The new building was not expected to be ready for occupancy till the following year. The EJC threatened further protests if the matter remained unresolved. A delegation from the Foreign Affairs Committee of the Board of Deputies had attended the meeting and reported on its findings in January 1992.

On reading the report, Sternberg contacted a number of high-ranking Catholics, including some of the Geneva signatories, alerting them to the possibility of a delay in the completion of the centre. In February he received two important communications, both of which suggested that the schedule for construction work remained on track. Writing on behalf of Cardinal Decourtray, Father Jean Dujardin, Secretary of the French Bishops' Committee, provided an up-to-date account of the situation. Dujardin had attended the cornerstone-laying ceremony and emphasized how important it was to demonstrate to Polish public opinion, which had remained uneasy about the removal of the convent, that both the Church and the Holy Father, himself, were unshakeable in their resolve that the transfer should take place.

Dujardin, who was also President of the International Programming Council for the Auschwitz Centre, had found the administrative building of the future centre nearing completion on his visit and believed that the construction of the convent was progressing smoothly. He expressed concern, however, that delays might be caused by a possible shortfall in financing.

Sternberg's second correspondent was Father Marek Glownia of the Auschwitz Foundation. In an upbeat letter he gave notice that the administrative building was now completed and that a symposium for journalists would be held there at the end of February. This was to be on the subject of 'Nationalism and Patriotism in Contemporary Europe' with a distinguished cast of speakers from Poland and other European countries. The new convent, Glownia hoped, would be ready for the sisters to move into by the end of the year.

More disturbing was an article published at the time by Stefan Wilkanowicz and sent to Sternberg by Glownia's assistant, Sylvia Temple. In his discussion on 'Neo-nazis, Revisionists and Gas Chambers', Wilkanowicz pointed out that Holocaust deniers frequently visited Auschwitz with the intention of inflaming Catholic–Jewish tensions. These so-called revisionists were zealous in their defence of the Carmelite sisters who, they claimed, were persecuted by the Jews.

The objectives of the 'revisionists' were facilitated by the fact that the museum and exhibitions at Auschwitz did not reflect the reality of the Holocaust and barely acknowledged the suffering of the Jews. This was a finding that emerged from a symposium of Jewish academics on the future of the Auschwitz–Birkenau site. Organized by the Oxford academic Jonathan Webber, in his role as principal coordinator of the Yarnton Group of Jewish Intellectuals concerned with the future of Auschwitz (which held its first meeting in 1990, in the Yarnton campus of the Oxford Centre for Hebrew and Jewish Studies), this symposium was held in collaboration with the Research Centre on Jewish History and Culture at the Jagiellonian University, Cracow (of which Webber was a Senior Research Fellow) and partially funded by the Polish Ministry of Culture. The delegates at the symposium noted that the Jewish pavilion at the Auschwitz museum was small and in a poor state of repair. A $45 million conservation programme for Birkenau was recommended.

One positive development in May was the establishment by the Polish government of a foundation of 'Eternal Commemoration'. This was set up with the aim of preserving the cemeteries and buildings which were part of Poland's Jewish heritage and providing cultural and educational programmes to promote Polish–Jewish links. Since President Walesa had faced complaints on his visit to Israel the previous year about the derelict condition of Jewish monuments in Poland, this was a sign that the Polish government was sensitive to outside pressure on certain issues.

Matters regarding the convent, however, were outside the government's preserve. And by July 1992, Sternberg's patience was wearing thin. In a letter to Stanislaw Krajewski, who had just been elected to the Executive of the International Council of Christians and Jews, he asked for up-to-date information on the building of the new centre.

The beginning of July had witnessed a sad loss to the cause of Christian–Jewish understanding with the death from heart failure of Rabbi Marc Tanenbaum. Tanenbaum, who was only 66, had worked tirelessly to foster dialogue and reconciliation while promoting Jewish involvement in the life of the nation and helping Christians to be better informed about Jewish history, culture and religion. From his writings on the subject, it would appear that the dispute over the Auschwitz convent was a subject he had taken to heart and it is sad that he did not live to witness the final departure of the Carmelites.

A sobering appraisal of the situation from a Polish perspective was to be found in an article published in *Occasional Papers on Religion in Eastern Europe* the following month. In the paper on Catholic–Jewish dialogue in Poland, Waldemar Chrostowski spoke of the detrimental effect the convent dispute had had on the dialogue between the Church and the Jews. While Chrostowski regarded Cardinal Macharski's 'unprecedented decision to move the convent to another place' as a sign of friendliness towards Jews, he went on to point out that 'the issue of moving the nuns is still a subject of lively debate. I believe the sisters themselves, on whose attitude depends the happy resolution of the bitter conflict, have the most to say about this'. Chrostowski's words were to prove particularly significant.

This was something Sternberg was to discover for himself when, at the invitation of the Polish government, he visited Poland with his wife in the last week of August. Whether or not he had read Chrostowski's article at the time, he had decided to take a proactive stance and intended to arrange a meeting with the Carmelite prioress, Sister Teresa. When the Sternbergs arrived at Auschwitz, they were received by Father Marek Glownia, the director of the new centre. The centre was already open but the new convent nearby where the Carmelites were to be housed was not complete. Although building work was in progress, it was not clear when the convent would be open, particularly as the winter was approaching.

Father Glownia preferred not to accompany the Sternbergs on their visit to Sister Teresa but arranged for his assistant, Sylvia Tempel, to go with them and act as an interpreter. As an introduction, Sternberg pushed a photograph through the grille on the convent door showing him in full Knight Commander's regalia together with Pope John Paul II. Whether or not this had the desired effect, it appeared that the often recalcitrant prioress was appreciative of the 'calm and friendly attitude' displayed by the conciliatory papal knight. However, she could not see the presence of the Carmelites at the new centre 'as consistent with the sisters' vocation'.

Since the sisters belonged to an enclosed order and were unable to leave the convent and inspect the new building, Sternberg arranged for a model of the new convent to be built at his expense, which could be displayed inside the existing convent. He hoped to soften the nuns' attitude to the move by enabling them to acquire some familiarity with the new building and was not to know that his proposal would itself generate extensive correspondence and no little confusion. Eventually the idea of a model had to be abandoned as it turned out to be too expensive. In its place Sternberg commissioned an architect's drawing of the new convent. This was presented some months later to Sister Teresa who promptly rejected it.

In Poland Sternberg also met Cardinal Glemp and discussed with him the formation of an advisory committee for the new centre. He and his wife spent the Sabbath in Warsaw, where both the chief rabbi and, in his turn, Stanislaw Krajewski, affirmed the importance of co-operation as a means of achieving results. It was clear that the Polish Jews feared a backlash of anti-Semitism if anything were to take place at Auschwitz that might provoke adverse reaction. On returning to London, Sternberg contacted the Carmelites in Rome and was told that the matter was in the hands of Cardinals Cassidy and Glemp.

Some weeks later, Sternberg had talks with the two cardinals at a meeting of the St Egidio in Louvain. Both reaffirmed statements made in September 1989. Glemp stood by 'his' letter of 20 September stating that the Geneva declaration should be implemented while Cassidy reiterated the Vatican Commission statement made by his predecessor which stressed that the prayer and dedicated life of the Carmelite sisters would contribute decisively to the success of the new centre. One absentee at Louvain was Cardinal Macharski of Cracow, who had been unable to attend because of ill health.

9. Late 1992:
Gridlock

September 1992 found Catholics and Jews ostensibly united as to the desirability of the Carmelites' relocating. Building work on the new convent was continuing apace. Yet whether there was any real likelihood of the sisters making the move remained uncertain, if not doubtful. Whereas this may not have been apparent to those who were distant from the scene, Sternberg's Polish initiative highlighted the extent to which the aims of the Catholic–Jewish consensus were dependent on the Carmelite Superior. His mission also served as a catalyst to the varied interpretations and expectations of the many parties involved, whether in Poland or abroad, and these gave rise to no little degree of misunderstanding, as a flurry of correspondence reveals.

The Chief Rabbi of Poland, Pinchas Menachem Joskowicz, regarded the battle to remove the sisters as a 'lost cause'. He had been told, he wrote to Sternberg on 4 September, that there was no authority that could move them. The rabbi outlined a grim scenario of a future after all survivors of the Holocaust had passed away: 'If a Catholic Convent is permitted to remain in this place, in 20 years' time one could believe that Jews were never here in Auschwitz.'

Joskowicz requested Sternberg's support for a proposal that would provide for a Jewish presence at Auschwitz. He planned to establish a seminary in an old synagogue in Cracow where 30 students could live and study for three months at a time. The students would travel to Auschwitz three times a week and would study *Mishnayot* – portions from the Mishna, which is the Oral Law – on the ruins of the crematorium in memory of the Jews murdered there.

The obstinacy of the Carmelites was also the subject of an article in *The Times* of 5 September by Clifford Longley, himself a Catholic, who spoke of the nuns as 'a law unto themselves'. In an impassioned peroration, Longley accused the Mother Superior, Sister Teresa, of acting in an unloving way:

Her vocation is prayer and that is the sole purpose of her presence at Auschwitz. Prayer *is* charity. Unloving, uncharitable prayer is a contradiction: God does not listen to it. While she stays where she is, she is wasting her time, contrary to the rule of her order, her vocation and the example of her namesake, Teresa of Avila.

Longley's article was quickly put to use by Sternberg, who sent it to many of the interested parties. In an emollient letter to Sister Teresa, thanking her for the courteous reception she had accorded him and his wife, he also enclosed a copy of the article and enjoined the Carmelite Superior to let him have her reaction.

Not surprisingly, Sternberg's habit of taking unilateral initiatives made him vulnerable to criticism. In a personal fax message of 8 September, Gerhart Riegner of the WJC took him to task for his Polish exploits. Riegner, who appeared to have a much more optimistic view of recent developments at Auschwitz than Sternberg, claimed that the information he had received based on 'very serious sources' in Rome, Paris and Poland was very different from what Sternberg had reported in a press release on his Polish trip. Riegner had been assured by his sources that all financial problems had been solved and that all necessary steps had been prepared to ensure the departure of the Carmelites after the new convent building was completed. Many of the nuns were expected to return to their former convents. In the meantime, the Jewish world had been asked to keep quiet.

'Under these circumstances I do not see any reason for your recent visit nor for your press release, nor for your encounters with the Prioress of the convent in Auschwitz or with Cardinal Glemp,' Riegner wrote. 'This whole matter is so delicate that I strongly ask you to consult with me prior to taking any further initiative on this problem.' He went on to suggest that in consulting with the Polish primate, Sternberg was 'upgrading' him since recent reforms introduced by the Polish episcopate had deprived Glemp of some of his previous prerogatives. Riegner also reported that 'our friend' Muszynski had been made archbishop of the prestigious diocese of Gniezno and might well become the next primate of Poland.

Sternberg was bemused by the contradictory reports he had received regarding the financing of the new convent and centre. Here was Riegner convinced that all was in order whereas Father Glownia had told him of a shortfall of $700,000. To clarify the situation he contacted Glownia immediately and received a prompt reply to the effect that whereas $300,000 was available and could provide for the most basic amenities for the new convent which would enable the nuns to move by the end of the year, a further $700,000 would be needed to finish the convent, build a chapel and put the finishing touches to the new centre.

At the same time Glownia contacted Théo Klein in Paris and gave him a brief résumé of Sternberg's visit to the convent and the current financial situation. In his letter to Klein, he explained that building delays had been due in part to inadequate financing and made it clear that while sufficient funds were now in hand to provide accommodation for the sisters, much more money would be needed to complete the project. Since the $300,000 had been made available through the good offices of Father Jean Dujardin, with whom he would have been familiar, and since Glownia had not spelt out the shortfall as explicitly as he had to Sternberg, it is not surprising, perhaps, that Klein, too, took the optimistic view that the financial matters had been resolved.

A less sanguine correspondent was Father Camilo Maccise, the Carmelite Superior General, who had been informed of Sternberg's visit to Auschwitz on his return to Rome. While he expressed gratitude for Sternberg's interest in resolving the problem of the Auschwitz convent and his 'all-embracing and open attitude', he made it clear that his own influence was limited:

> I hold no direct authority over the Discalced Carmelite Nuns. It is not I who erects or suppresses their Monasteries, but rather the Congregation of Religious ... I would like to repeat that I, as Superior General of the Carmelites, have tried to contribute to the dialogue and the solution of the problem. More than this I am not able to do.

Sternberg replied to Riegner on 11 September. His letter was unusually blunt, possibly in order to strip his colleague of the illusion that all was smooth sailing on the Auschwitz front. He made a point of emphasizing the $700,000 shortfall. 'So much hinges on this question of money – without which the new Convent cannot be completed and the move of the nuns take place – that it is crucial for the situation to be clarified.' He went on to stress that Sister Teresa had left him in no doubt that the nuns were not prepared to move. 'She is a law unto herself and a political animal to boot,' he wrote, recognizing an adversary when he found one.

Since Riegner was also due to visit Poland at the end of the month, Sternberg recommended that he should meet the Mother Superior as well as Rabbi Joskowicz. The views of Polish Jews needed to be taken into account for, as he put it, 'the Jewish community in Poland is in the firing line'. He also urged Riegner to give his support to the new Advisory Committee he had formed with Cardinal Glemp, on which, for the first time, the Carmelites would be represented.

A statement released by Cardinal Glemp at this point reiterates the 'relevance' of creating a permanent board which could supervise the development of the new centre. In this statement the Polish primate reported on the meeting he had had with Sternberg in Poland and disclosed that the newly formed committee would also include representatives from the Vatican and from Israel. He announced, too, that he had accepted an invitation to visit the Sternberg Centre for Judaism on his forthcoming visit to London in October. Glemp's prospective visit and the chance it would provide for further discussions with Sternberg gave rise to a certain optimism in Polish diplomatic circles, among others, that maybe now a solution might be found to the 'very important problem' of the Carmelites at Auschwitz.

A fresh controversy involving Auschwitz was about to erupt. Reports that the Polish government was planning to charge entrance fees to the Auschwitz museum and for admission to Auschwitz–Birkenau were giving rise to consternation in some Jewish quarters. The Speaker of the Israeli Knesset, Shevach Weiss, complained vociferously to President Walesa that the proposal to raise money for the upkeep of the structures at the death camps was 'nightmarish and surrealistic'. These reports were later denied by the Polish embassy in Tel Aviv although it was acknowledged that 'disastrous financial conditions' had prompted the Polish authorities to consider ways of raising money.

By mid-September the complex financial arrangements surrounding the building of the new centre and convent had become common knowledge to the many interested parties. While Cardinal Cassidy, head of the Vatican's Commission for Religious Relations with Judaism, was confident that funds were available to complete the new convent building, he was unsure as to how the shortfall for the completion of the centre might be remedied. Nevertheless Cassidy, the Vatican's representative in its relations with the Jews, was unequivocal in affirming that the Carmelites would have to leave the existing convent.

Sternberg, who saw Cassidy as a 'very good friend', was aware nonetheless that the patience of the Jewish world was being considerably stretched, particularly as there now appeared to be no time limit imposed on the nuns vacating the old theatre building. As he informed Israel Singer of the WJC in New York, he had met Belgian Jews during his visit to Louvain for the St Egidio meeting who were clearly unhappy with the current situation. He appealed to Singer to communicate the necessity of patience. 'The reality is that we have to leave it to the Vatican to get on with it and we should not make any public statement.' In accordance with the need for quiet diplomacy rather than public protest, the President of the Board of Deputies,

Judge Israel Finestein, wrote privately to Cardinals Glemp and Cassidy expressing the growing concern of the Jewish world.

Sternberg had also updated representatives of the European Jewish Congress as to how things stood following his visit to Poland and his meetings with Cardinals Glemp and Cassidy in Louvain. Doubtless bearing in mind the words of Polish Chief Rabbi Joskowicz that the battle to remove the Carmelites from the convent was a 'lost cause', an idea had occurred to him that rabbinical authorities might declare that the existing convent was outside the death camp's perimeter. This he had floated in his communiqué to the EJC. On learning from Serge Cwajgenbaum, Secretary General of the EJC, that this 'proposal' was quite unacceptable, he urged Cwajgenbaum to use his good offices to convince the Polish chief rabbi of the Vatican's determination that the nuns should move.

Inevitably, Sternberg's independent mode of operation was again called into question. To what extent his critics were motivated by doubts about the wisdom of his course of action or by organizational or interpersonal rivalry is not clear. What is apparent is that the EJC with its established procedures was concerned at the ventures into uncharted territory undertaken by this Jewish 'loose cannon'. This time it was Théo Klein in Paris who was obliged to remind him, albeit gently, that Father Dujardin was involved in the day-to-day running of the Carmelite affair and preferred not to have too many people working on the issue without co-operating with him.

Sternberg promptly contacted Dujardin and sent him the report on his Polish visit he had presented to the Board of Deputies and circulated to all the parties involved. The report was the subject of a further animated, yet not unfriendly, batch of correspondence from Théo Klein. What stuck in the throat of Klein and his colleagues was the fact that a Jew should have broken the voluntary boycott the EJC had imposed with regard to direct contact with Sister Teresa, known as a troublemaker who deliberately made contradictory statements to different visitors. Where Sternberg asserted that the sisters complained that they had never been consulted about their future, Klein saw this as the task of Cardinal Macharsky, Archbishop of the local diocese, and 'certainly not the role of the Jewish party'.

The EJC had also received a briefing from Father Marek Glownia in Poland. The director of the new centre hinted at the recalcitrance of the Carmelite prioress, Sister Teresa, regarding the move which had been evident during her meeting with Sternberg. He reiterated, however, that the personal opinions of the prioress could not invalidate the Vatican's declaration of 19 September 1989. Glownia also commented on the centre's finances and was less ambiguous than before in declaring that further means of financing were actively being sought.

To the many voices in the Catholic and Jewish worlds united in their approach to the Carmelite presence at Auschwitz, that of Basil Hume must be added. The Cardinal Archbishop of Westminster had discussed the matter on a visit to Rome and had been assured that 'many persons in high places in Rome' agreed that 'some action simply must be taken'. Hume had also been told that the new bishop of the diocese in which the convent was located was 'entirely in favour' of the convent being removed.

That this consensus of *bien pensants* might not reflect the attitude of the 'man in the street' became evident when Polish expatriates took to the correspondence columns of the British press. A particularly well-argued letter in the *Evening Standard* of 22 September made a point that continues to be relevant:

> One can perhaps understand that the Jewish people may choose not to pray at the Golgotha of their nation 'because God was silent when their people were dying'. This is their choice. But they shouldn't seek to impose this attitude on others who may choose different ways of cherishing their dead. Why shouldn't a few Polish nuns be left in peace to pray for the Polish dead on Polish soil?

This very reasonable argument accentuated the desirability of some visible Jewish presence or symbol in the vicinity of Auschwitz that would not be provided by the facilities of the new centre. Indeed in a report on his visit to Auschwitz of 24 September, Sigmund Sobolewski, a former Polish Catholic prisoner who had spent four-and-a-half years in the camp, deplored the absence of Jewish memorabilia. 'Why does Poland still downplay the martyrdom of 1.6 million Jews murdered in Auschwitz?' he wrote.

For the Jewish side, both Jonathan Webber and Rabbi Joskowicz had made this point, although the proposals they had put forward were very different. Now with the approach of yet another deadline for the move of the Carmelites with little hope of being met, Webber sent Sternberg a new proposal for an independent Jewish house in Oswiecim to cater for the increased flow of Jewish visitors. Writing as a member of the International Auschwitz Council and chairman of its standing committee on education, he also asked whether the Jewish world might agree to the old theatre building being used as exhibition space once the Carmelites had left.

While Sternberg's response to the proposed 'Jewish House' was lukewarm, he endorsed the idea that the vacated convent should be transformed into a museum. Fearing that this might be a minority view, he urged Webber to canvass the idea, explaining that the nuns might be more likely to leave if the premises they were vacating were to be used for a specific purpose. To this effect a draft text was prepared and circulated to various Jewish organizations in the hope of gaining support.

In the meantime the new Auschwitz centre had hosted a meeting of its International Programme Council chaired by Father Dujardin and attended by prominent members from abroad. Among these were Monsignor Pier Francesco Fumagalli representing the Vatican Conference for Dialogue with Judaism and Gerhart Riegner representing the IJCIC. Further activities in the autumn of 1992 included a talk by the author and Holocaust survivor Halina Birenbaum and a visit from a group of young people from Israel. However, as the centre's director, Father Glownia, acknowledged in a letter to Sternberg, 'the situation of the Carmelite Sisters is a most delicate one'. The centre was relying on the new bishop of the diocese and local priests to prepare the sisters to accept their move to the new convent.

In another attempt to achieve the same end, Father Oliver McTernan, a parish priest in London, had contacted the mother superior of a Carmelite convent in his diocese and asked her to write to the prioress at Auschwitz urging the sisters to move to the new convent. Initially Sister Mary, the Superior, had been reluctant to do so, believing that there was no evidence that Sister Teresa had refused to move. After further persistence, however, Father McTernan was able to convince her. Meanwhile a report in the *Catholic Herald* focusing on the unresolved situation at Auschwitz prompted Sternberg to contact Cardinal Cassidy from whom he had received information that seemed much more hopeful.

A more positive interlude late in October was the long-awaited visit of Cardinal Glemp to the Sternberg Centre in London. This passed very successfully and prompted the cardinal to send Sternberg an effusive letter of thanks, in which he expressed gratitude for being exposed to 'the richness of Jewish thought' and for sharing a meal with 'the excellent representatives of the Jewish Nation'. Glemp had also been shown a Torah scroll to which he responded 'with great emotion'. He concluded his letter in the hope that 'Oswiecim would really be the Centre of Information, Meetings, Dialogue, Education and Prayer'.

By November, however, the centre itself appeared to be undergoing yet another financial crisis. As its operating costs exceeded its income, Father Glownia was forced to suspend orders for fixtures and fittings and to give notice to his employees. On receiving this information from Glownia, Sternberg contacted Théo Klein in Paris, who passed on his communication to Father Dujardin for him to deal with. Sternberg also contacted Gerhart Riegner who suggested that the American Catholic Church should be approached to make a financial contribution.

The new convent, in contrast, which had been financed primarily by benefactors in France, was now nearing completion. Yet for all the comforts and amenities it offered, there appeared little likelihood that the Carmelite Sisters would move. In view of the delicate situation, the co-chairmen of the Polish Council of Christians and Jews, Waldemar Chrostowski and Stanislaw Krajewski, offered the Council's help and expertise both to officials of the new centre and to Cardinal Glemp's office but the offer was not taken up. Moreover, as Krajewski reported to Sternberg, other members of the Polish CCJ were not inclined to help: 'They feel we should not do the work for those who started the whole process and neglected the nuns, thereby making the process more and more painful and full of conflicts' – yet another indictment, it would appear, of the role of the Polish Church hierarchy in the convent affair.

Despite this continuing impasse, Catholic–Jewish relations were cemented at the end of the year by two prominent awards. In November Gerhart Riegner was conferred with the insignia of Knight, Commander of St Gregory the Great by Cardinal Cassidy in a ceremony at the Pontifical Lateran University. And the following month Sternberg received the Commander Cross of the Order of Merit of the Republic of Poland. Both men had worked tirelessly in their different ways for the promotion of dialogue and for a solution to the convent crisis.

1. Supporter of crosses holds banner in front of Auschwitz Block II. (*Chris Schwarz/Aspect Picture Library*).

2. Switon carrying cross. (*Chris Schwarz/Aspect Picture Library*).

3. Father Adolph Chojnacki conducting a Mass. (*Chris Schwarz/Aspect Picture Library*).

4. Lady kneeling in prayer at site of crosses. (*Chris Schwarz/Aspect Picture Library*).

5. Members of the national radical young patriots (skinheads) carrying their crosses. (*Chris Schwarz/Aspect Picture Library*).

6. Woman kissing the original cross commemorating the Pope's first visit to Poland. (*Chris Schwarz/Aspect Picture Library*).

7. National radical young patriots pose by the entrance gate at Auschwitz. (*Chris Schwarz/Aspect Picture Library*).

8. Portrait of priest who conducted a controversial Mass supporting crosses. (*Chris Schwarz/Aspect Picture Library*).

10. Early 1993:
An End in Sight?

The new year dawned with yet another controversy on the Auschwitz horizon when Hollywood director Steven Spielberg asked to use the camp as a backdrop for shooting scenes for his new film, *Schindler's List*. Spielberg's request which, it was believed, would have involved bringing hundreds of extras, erecting a fake gas chamber and crematorium in Birkenau and monopolizing the site for a few days, was turned down by the Auschwitz Museum on the advice of the International Auschwitz Council but this decision was overruled by the Polish Ministry of Culture.

This new imposition which, according to Jonathan Webber, had 'horrified and demoralized' the Museum staff, was deeply unwelcome to much of the Jewish world. As Webber pointed out in a letter to Kalman Sultanik of the WJC, the Spielberg project would not only 'constitute a serious desecration of the grounds of Auschwitz', but would prompt the Polish and international media to 'make mincemeat of Jewish concern about Auschwitz and in particular Jewish objections to the Carmelite convent'.

Once again major Jewish organizations, with the notable exception of the Simon Wiesenthal Centre, which saw no objection to the project, were at war over the status of Auschwitz. The irony was that this time their opponent was one of their own co-religionists. To compound the irony, an official of the WJC travelled to Poland to ask the Warsaw government to change its decision and Jewish groups in Washington asked the Polish ambassador to convey their protests to his government. 'Our concern is the dignity of a place which is the largest Jewish burial ground in the world ... We do not want it turned into a Hollywood back lot,' a WJC spokesman explained.

No less ironic was the letter sent by Sternberg to Cardinal Glemp, asking him to 'use your great influence in religious and lay quarters to prevent a course of action which can only be harmful to Christian–Jewish relations'. This occasioned a headline 'Sternberg v. Spielberg in Auschwitz Movie Row' in the following edition of the *Jewish Chronicle*.

But for all the puff and bluster, the numerous letters and articles
on the subject from many quarters, this was no more than a storm in
a teacup, a mere microcosm of the seemingly never-ending struggle
over the Carmelite convent. Spielberg soon agreed to meet with Sultanik
of the WJC to hammer out details of a compromise. A few days later
Sternberg was involved in a debate on the BBC World Service with
Spielberg's co-director, Branko Lustig, himself a survivor of Auschwitz.
Lustig promised that nothing would be done during the two-and-a-half
days filming at Auschwitz which would cause offence.

In the event, Spielberg agreed to shoot scenes from the film outside
the grounds of Auschwitz rather than within the death camp. The
sequence would be filmed in black and white in documentary style.
Expressing satisfaction with the outcome, Sternberg wrote to Spielberg
suggesting that the premieres of *Schindler's List* in Britain and Germany
should be under the auspices of the respective Councils of Christians
and Jews.

The Spielberg episode, which was resolved by the middle of February,
may have provided a welcome diversion from the seemingly intractable
Carmelite saga. An information bulletin put out in January 1993 by
the Executive Board of the Auschwitz Centre disclosed that the residential section and the enclosure wall of the new convent had been
completed, providing accommodation for '20 contemplative sisters'.
The section for worship, the outdoor surroundings and the balance of
the residential section would be completed during 1993. The first of the
buildings for the centre itself was complete and future buildings were
planned. The tone of the bulletin gave the impression, contrary to Father
Glownia's communication the previous autumn, that it was business as
usual. Indeed, another meeting of the centre's International Programme
Council had taken place, with Fumagalli and Riegner again present.

The bulletin made it clear, however, that the Executive Board was not
responsible for vacating the old theatre. It expressed the hope, however, that various national and local organizations would co-operate in
arriving at a satisfactory solution for the future of the gravel pit and
the old theatre once the Carmelites had left.

The frustration to which the protracted convent saga had given rise
spilled over in an outspoken outburst at a meeting of the Board of
Deputies in February. A representative claimed that the problem with
the convent was that the Jewish representation on the issue had been
'hijacked by the CCJ and Sir Sigmund Sternberg'. It was left to
the president, Judge Finestein, to defend Sternberg's conscientious
efforts to seek a resolution.

By early March, however, Sternberg himself felt that further action
was needed. On this he was at one with Gerhart Riegner, who had

recently returned from Rome where he had received scant satisfaction. The two men met at a consultation of the ICCJ Executive in Heppenheim chaired by Sternberg, where they received confirmation from Dr Stefan Schreiner of the German CCJ and his Polish counterpart, Stanislaw Krajewski, that although the new convent was ready for occupation the Carmelites showed no signs of moving. The Heppenheim meeting was also attended by Father Remi Hoeckman, the Vatican representative on the ICCJ, to whom Sternberg and Riegner expressed their feelings of exasperation. Sternberg then proposed that a consultation should be set up between himself, Finestein, Riegner and Israel Singer of the WJC by way of an international telephone conference call to discuss a letter that would be sent to Hoeckman.

The conference consultation took place on Friday, 5 March and the following Monday Sternberg wrote to Hoeckman, enclosing Clifford Longley's article of the previous September. Recalling the concern Riegner had expressed after his visit to Rome, Sternberg pointed out that the growing seriousness of the convent situation not only threatened to damage Jewish–Catholic relations but, more importantly, to undermine the credibility of the Vatican itself if the Vatican was seen to be unable to enforce its instructions. Sternberg's own reputation was also on the line in view of his continued initiatives to solve the convent crisis.

Sternberg also enclosed a report from the latest edition of the *Jewish Chronicle* stating that the European Jewish Congress was threatening to boycott the fiftieth anniversary commemorations of the Warsaw Ghetto Uprising if the nuns had not moved. The ceremony was scheduled to take place on 19 April. In view of the threatened boycott he gave 17 April as a deadline for the Carmelites to move and explained that in this he was joined by Riegner, Finestein and Singer. 'It is inconceivable that the nuns should not be willing to say their prayers a few hundred yards away, but insist on staying in the largest Jewish cemetery in the world when this offends susceptibilities so profoundly', Sternberg wrote.

Hoeckman's reply was prompt but terse. Touching on the Auschwitz convent he alluded to 'certain canonical procedures' which needed to be followed. 'A lot of motion does not help us in any way' was his conclusion. Drafting a reply in conjunction with Finestein, Sternberg asked Hoeckman to clarify, 'as a matter of urgency', the reference to 'canonical procedures'. Acknowledging the Vatican representative's point about 'a lot of motion', Sternberg pointed to the 'mounting anxiety' among the Jewish community about the 'inexplicable delay'.

By now the Jewish world was divided over the issue of 'to boycott or not to boycott'. The WJC was in consultation with the government of

Israel over the issue and Edgar Bronfman, the WJC president, had decided to write to the Pope. The Polish government, sensitive to the damage that the proposed boycott would inflict on the commemoration ceremony and on Poland's good name, dispatched Dr Zakrzewski, Minister in the President's Chancellery, to see Sister Teresa.

Sternberg was one of the opponents of the boycott. After consulting Ben Helfgott, a Holocaust survivor and Chairman of the Institute for Polish–Jewish Studies, he argued that the Polish government could not be blamed for failing to relocate the Carmelites. Jonathan Webber, too, considered such action not only to be misguided but counter-productive. In addition to his involvement at board level with both the Museum and the Centre at Auschwitz, Webber had by this time been working with the Jagiellonian University in Cracow for seven years on major Polish–Jewish educational projects and had witnessed at first hand the development of fruitful Jewish–Christian and Polish–Jewish dialogue and reconciliation at the local level.

The case against the boycott was presented compellingly by Aubrey Rose, a Vice-President of the Board of Deputies. In a paper on the subject, Rose compared the Carmelite sisters with their 'mentality of fanatical extremists, totally sincere, believing their action is com-pletely justified, doing God's will, saving souls' to the Catholics of the Inquisition, the IRA and Muslim fundamentalists. Rather than a boy-cott, which would demean world Jewry and give propaganda value to anti-Semites, Rose suggested a joint Catholic–Jewish prayer gathering directed at the Carmelites:

> We have to shame the nuns on spiritual grounds. If their God, as ours, is everywhere, then prayer, wherever it takes place, is just as valid. Their prayers will be just as effective in the new building as in their present building. We should all pray for the nuns that their eyes be opened to the suffering they are causing here to others.

As March turned to April with the threatened boycott making waves in the Polish and international media, a last-ditch attempt was devised to resolve the convent crisis. As reported in the *Jewish Chronicle* of 2 April, Polish bishops had approached the Vatican's Sacred Congre-gation of Religious, which oversees monastic orders, to issue a formal directive to persuade the nuns to move. By the following day, over-optimistically perhaps, *The Times* and the *Independent* reported that the nuns would move.

The Polish bishops' action did not escape controversy, given that the majority of the Polish faithful were believed to have viewed the Geneva agreements as capitulation in the face of Jewish protest. In fact, as reported in *The Catholic World Report*, Waldemar Chrostowski himself publicly accused the bishops of failing to explain their decision to the Polish people, 'who view Auschwitz with as much emotion as the Jews'.

Although the Congregation of the Religious did, in fact, take steps to dissolve the Carmelite community, thereby enabling the nuns to leave, it appears that this was not enough. According to a Vatican spokesman, the sisters had asked 'informally' to know what the Pope's position was on the matter.

In the event the Pope, himself, was obliged to intervene. This, as Gerhart Riegner saw it, was the decisive moment. 'Now, in conformity with the will of the Church, you will change your place while remaining in the same town of Auschwitz,' John-Paul II wrote to the sisters. 'This will be for each of you, a moment of trial. I pray that Christ crucified will help you to know His will and the particular vocation for each of you in the Carmelite life.'

The papal letter was dated 9 April and was received on 10 April although it was not made public until 15 April. There is speculation that the nuns initially balked as key figures in the Polish Church met at Auschwitz on the day of the letter's arrival. These included Cardinal Macharski and Father Glownia, while the task of enforcing the Vatican's instructions was left to the local bishop, Monseigneur Tadeusz Rakoczy. Once the letter was made public, Racoczy announced that, 'The Carmelite sisters in Auschwitz fully submit to the will of the Holy Father'. Some parties in Auschwitz, however, circulated a petition expressing opposition to moving the convent.

The Pope's intervention enabled the Warsaw Ghetto commemoration to go ahead with full Jewish participation, although it was not until late May that the first five nuns moved to the new convent. On Monday, 24 May the new convent was blessed by Bishop Rakoczy in the course of a modest ceremony attended only by the sisters and a few priests. The bishop also celebrated the first mass at the new centre. Journalists reporting from the new centre were given to understand that funds were greatly stretched and that financial help was being sought from the Catholic Church in Western countries.

At the end of May Sternberg and his wife became the first visitors from abroad to call at the new complex. Reporting on his visit to Father Dujardin in Paris, he informed him that no building work was going on at the centre due to a lack of funds although the materials were already on site. In his reply Dujardin promised to make a note of the financial situation on his next visit a few weeks later.

The peripatetic Sternberg had returned to Poland to receive the 'Man of Reconciliation' award from the Polish Council of Christians and Jews. Earlier, as ever in pursuit of greater understanding, he had visited Rome where he had called on the Carmelite Superior General. Before the presentation, Sternberg was welcomed by co-chairman Waldemar Chrostowski who recalled his meeting with Cardinal Glemp in 1989 and his persistent advocacy of dialogue as the only way to improve mutual relations. Chrostowski also cited the message from the Polish president read out at the presentation ceremony in London when Sternberg had been awarded the Commander's Cross the previous year: 'Due to your initiative, the Centre for Dialogue and Prayer in Oswiecim has been established.'

At the centre, the Sternbergs were taken by Father Glownia to meet Sister Maria, who was in charge of the new convent. Sternberg presented her with a medal commemorating the fiftieth Anniversary of the Warsaw Ghetto Uprising.

The remaining nine Carmelite sisters were obliged to leave the 'old theatre' building by the end of June. Even this deadline was not met, although on 30 June Bishop Rakoczy issued a decree de-consecrating the chapel and opening the building for secular purposes. It was only on 6 July that the building adjacent to the concentration camp which had been a source of contention for nine years was finally vacated. Rather than move to the new convent, the sisters left Oswiecim.

11. 1993 Onwards:
The Superior's Revenge

Already in its report of 2 April, the *Jewish Chronicle* had quoted Father Marek Glownia as saying that he foresaw problems with the removal of the cross in the convent garden. This was picked up by Sternberg who reported on the matter to Israel Singer and Gerhart Riegner. With hindsight it would appear that Glownia was remarkably prescient.

No further information on the matter came to light while the Carmelites remained in the old theatre. However, at the beginning of July, news filtered out of a development that was equally disturbing. Instead of returning the old theatre to the Oswiecim council, which had leased the building to the nuns on condition that it would be used as a contemplative monastery, the Mother Superior, Sister Teresa, had given a cheap 30-year lease to a militant Polish organization, the Polish War Victims Association. In a statement to the press, Miecyslaw Janosz, founder and chairman of the association, announced that the building would house an archive documenting the 'harm suffered by Poles through persecution by aggressors in 1939–45, as well as under post-war totalitarian governments'. According to Stanislaw Krajewski, Janosz and his brothers had been involved some years earlier in criminal activity involving robbing stores in western Europe, organized by Polish intelligence in conjunction with some leaders of the Communist Party.

While the association claimed that official Church representatives would be present at a ceremony to lay the first plaque in honour of Polish martyrs, Krajewski emphasized that the move was not supported by Church leaders or the local authorities. Indeed a report in *The Tablet* quoted Father Glownia protesting that the Mother Superior had no right to rent out the building.

The news came as a blow to Sternberg who had already expressed anxiety about what would happen to the vacated convent building. In June he had written to Ronald Lauder of the Lauder Foundation who was raising funds in order to preserve the remaining barracks at Auschwitz–Birkenau and suggested that Lauder include the old theatre building. 'There is a danger that the building will be vandalized or occupied by squatters', he had observed.

'Our shortcoming was that we did not put forward any plans of our own', Sternberg told the *Jewish Chronicle* after receiving the latest information from Krajewski. He passed on the information to Karel Drozd, director of the Polish Cultural Institute, and to his partners in consultation, Riegner, Singer and Finestein, and sent Glownia an urgent fax requesting further details.

While Drozd acknowledged that he would need more information from Poland before commenting, he expressed optimism that the situation would be resolved through legal conditions attached to the leasing of the building. Glownia's assistant, Sylvia Tempel, however, was far more cautious. Stating that 'immeasurable complication began' with the illegal leasing of the old theatre, she indicated that it was not clear whether the matter could be settled out of court.

In a fax to Sternberg which foreshadowed to a remarkable degree the source of future conflict, Tempel made a vital link between the new occupants of the former convent building and the relocation of the large papal cross. She explained that Bishop Rakoczy's plan to move the cross to the site of the new convent had been resisted by Oswiecim city council in view of the new complications.

Glownia, for his part, had obeyed the bishop's instructions and overseen the preparation of a foundation and concrete base for the cross at the new site. Contingency plans for the transportation of the cross had also been made. But as Tempel made clear, the centre's hands were tied. 'The resistance I described earlier exists outside the authoritative limits of the Catholic Church and outside the Cracow Foundation Centre of Information, Meetings, Dialogue, Education and Prayer in Auschwitz.' In a poignant personal reflection, Tempel confessed to feeling the 'pain of human helplessness, the moment when all human strength is weakness'.

Sternberg remained optimistic that the cross would, in fact, be resited and in early August wrote to Sylvia Tempel hoping that she could confirm that this had taken place. Tempel, however, could only confirm that nothing had changed since her earlier communication.

In the midst of the understandable frustration experienced by the Jewish officials who had waited so long for the convent crisis to be resolved, a note of reason and patience was struck by Jonathan Webber. In a letter to Sternberg, Webber indicated that any protest from Jewish organizations in connection with the cross would be counter-productive since not only had the Church honoured its commitment to relocate the convent, it had gone even further by deconsecrating the building. Furthermore, given the changes in Polish law since the fall of communism, there were major local difficulties in determining the precise legal ownership of the cross. The council of the new Centre, of which Webber was a member, had recently discussed the problem and it was clear that it would take time to resolve. Webber again emphasized the considerable improvements in Polish–Jewish relations both at the institutional and personal levels and brought up the fact that no definite plan for the future of the 'old theatre' building had been put forward.

In view of these developments and of the primary purpose of the Jewish world – 'to honour the sacred memory of those of our people who suffered and died in that appalling place' – Webber recommended that the Board of Deputies and other Jewish organizations should support the Auschwitz State Museum in its efforts to reflect the significance of the site in the context of the Holocaust. If the old theatre should pass into the Museum's care, it could be used for purposes consistent with that objective.

Webber had also warned that since Poland was in the midst of a general election campaign, anything said by Jews outside the country could be manipulated by the various political parties for their own ends. No such consideration, however, would prevent that veteran Auschwitz campaigner, Rabbi Avi Weiss, from having his say. Once it had become apparent that the Carmelites would vacate the old convent, Weiss had suggested that in deference to victims from all faiths, the area around Auschwitz should be free of either synagogues or churches. Since the cross would still be visible on churches within view of Auschwitz, the transfer of the Carmelites would not solve the problem.

What Weiss was really targeting was the church in Brzezinka which was located in a building built by prisoners for the SS in 1944 across the road from the Birkenau camp. In 1983 the Church took over the building and made it a parish church in the village. Many Jews may have agreed with Weiss that the presence of any church so close by was an attempt to 'dejudaise' the camp. Indeed Rabbi Marc Tanenbaum had made a reference to the church in an article for the *New York Times* in 1989. Krajewski, however, made a distinction between the church, which did not bother him, and the large papal cross which he regarded as 'an intrusion'.

It was over a year later, in August 1994, that Weiss put his words into action and led a delegation of ten to Auschwitz–Birkenau as well as to Sobibor and to Terezin in the Czech Republic. The delegation, which included women, were members of Amcha, the New York-based Coalition for Jewish Concerns. At Auschwitz–Birkenau, Weiss and his followers hung banners and protest notices outside the church and the large cross, claiming that the site of both the church and the cross violated the Geneva agreement under which religious symbols were to be removed. Polish Church officials contended, however, that the church and the cross, which commemorated the Christian victims of Auschwitz, were located outside the camp and were not in conflict with the Geneva accord.

The demonstration took place with police present. Although several residents of the area confronted the protesters and called for the removal of the banners, there were no scenes of violence on this occasion. After holding a prayer session, the delegation left the scene. 'I am not against religious symbols in places of worship but a cross or a church at Auschwitz is like a synagogue in a Catholic cemetery or a Jewish star in the Vatican square', Weiss explained in support of his demands that the offending symbols be moved.

Weiss and his followers were not alone in their protest. In an article in the international edition of *The Jerusalem Post* the following month on the apparent Christianization of Nazi concentration and death camps including Dachau, Sobibor and Terezin as well as Auschwitz–Birkenau, a visitor from Jerusalem complained that there were two crosses on the church at Birkenau: 'They dominate what must be the largest Jewish cemetery of all time. This is deliberate, blatant religious revisionism. It is Christianization of the Holocaust.'

The significance of these Christian symbols at Auschwitz was just one aspect of the larger question of what to do with the camp. Since the departure of the Carmelites, attention had been focused on the most effective way of ensuring that the lessons of Auschwitz should be preserved for the future. The Auschwitz Preservation Project under-written by the Ronald Lauder Foundation held a symposium at the site in August 1993 at the invitation of Jonathan Webber. The foundation had already secured pledges of money from several governments.

Over the next few months a number of articles on the subject appeared in broadsheets in Britain and America. Many of these articles featured comments from Webber, derived from his booklet *The Future of Auschwitz*, published in Oxford in 1992. Interest in the future of Auschwitz was fuelled in varying degrees by the opening of the Holocaust Museum in Washington, the screening of *Schindler's List* and the publication of the book *AUSCHWITZ, A History in Photographs*, with an English version prepared by Webber, together with Connie Wilsack (whom he was soon to marry).

The debate centred on whether it was preferable to preserve the existing, yet rapidly deteriorating remains of the physical infrastructure of the concentration and death camps, including a few post-war recon-structions, or to restore Auschwitz to what it had been. Since the Nazis had destroyed much of the evidence of their methods of extermination before they abandoned the camp, there were those who favoured restoration as a means of instructing future generations. On the other hand, there was the danger that the Holocaust denial industry would seize on any 'distortion' of Auschwitz for their own ends.

Yet another option, favoured by many in the Jewish world, was to leave the site to decay naturally, to fade into oblivion. 'Can you say Auschwitz lies in its meaning and not its physical site?' was a question Webber asked journalists as he walked over the floor of a gas chamber hastily reconstructed shortly after the Second World War. Auschwitz, said Webber, had to fulfil three functions: as a place of mourning, as a museum of record and, inevitably, as a tourist attraction. There was a need to steer a path between the 'theme park approach' and a dignified memorial.

Webber would have preferred all the exhibition material to be removed and put into an educational centre outside the camp. He was very conscious, too, of the lack of a Jewish memorial. 'The question is how to let Auschwitz sink into the European consciousness', he maintained. 'There should be a serious monument so that in 200 or 300 years there is something left to see. Otherwise I think the whole thing should be allowed to rot'.

Ideally, the Cracow Foundation Centre should have played a key part in the ongoing debate. However, as a letter from Glownia to Sternberg in February 1994 made clear, the situation of the foundation was plagued by persistent uncertainty. Such was the sad reality of this offshoot of the Geneva accords, for which the protagonists of interfaith dialogue had harboured such high hopes.

The centre was not the only casualty of the aspirations of Geneva. The Auschwitz declaration, *Zakhor*, drafted at the first Geneva meeting in 1986, had enjoined all to remember Auschwitz and Birkenau as the most potent symbols of the Nazi genocide of the Jews, and to remember, too, the others who had been murdered there. As the fiftieth anniversary of the liberation of Auschwitz–Birkenau approached, it became apparent that the precepts of *Zakhor* had been disregarded. This was the subject of intense dispute in December 1994 and early January 1995 between the Polish government and members of the WJC, who doubted whether the proposed ceremonies had properly acknowledged the Jewish significance of Auschwitz.

This consideration was also troubling Jonathan Webber who had been invited to participate in the organizing committee for the commemoration and had been sent a copy of the programme of events. In his reply to Andrzej Zakrzewski, Secretary of State in the President's Office, Webber pointed out that there was no mention of any specifically Jewish ritual act of remembrance at the principal remembrance ceremony. 'I should like to express the view that the absence of a Jewish ritual act of remembrance is seriously inappropriate on this occasion', Webber wrote. 'As a Jew and as an intellectual concerned with the historical truth, I confess myself shocked by your government's behaviour.'

Webber had been telephoned by various news agencies seeking an explanation of why a Jewish ritual act of remembrance was not the central feature of the commemoration ceremony. In the absence of a Jewish ceremony 'of proper weight and dignity', he believed that things were back to where they stood during the communist era 'when the central fact of Jewish martyrdom at Auschwitz was deliberately concealed through the device of referring instead to their respective nationalities'.

Webber's letter was written barely two weeks before the ceremony was due to take place, on 27 January 1995. Nevertheless he appealed to the Secretary of State to see that the 'simple error of judgement' was rectified:

> What is at stake, at one level, is Poland's international reputation in dealing justly with the commemoration of what you yourself have described as the worst sides of human nature. What is at stake at another and undoubtedly more important level, however, is for your government to show itself identifying with the dignity of one million Jewish victims whose ashes are scattered across these fields in a piece of your country.

Webber's powerful and passionate protest may have had some effect. Polish Chief Rabbi Menachem Joskowicz was, indeed, the first on the podium at the main public ceremony at Auschwitz on 27 January. However, he left immediately after he had completed his allocated four minutes of prayer, in order not to be associated with the rest of the proceedings, as his son later explained to Webber. As Webber remarked in an essay entitled '*Erinnern, Vergessen und Rekonstruktion der Vergangenheit*' in a publication on Auschwitz put out by the Fritz Bauer Institute, there was not a particularly large number of Jews present at the commemoration ceremonies and a noticeable absence of orthodox Jews.

The major Jewish figure at the ceremony was the Nobel Laureaute, Elie Wiesel, technically present as the representative of the president of the United States but regarded by many as the spokesperson of the survivors. The speaker of the Israeli Knesset also delivered a speech from the podium. Elsewhere, whether in the environs of Auschwitz–Birkenau or overseas, the occasion of the fiftieth-anniversary commemoration saw many of the key Jewish players in the Auschwitz saga acting out their traditional roles.

Sternberg, the conciliator, had written to the Polish president, Lech Walesa, congratulating the Poles on organizing the ceremony to which many heads of state had been invited. The WJC was represented by Kalman Sultanik, a vice-president, with the president, Edgar Bronfman, maintaining a diplomatic distance – possibly, as Webber's essay suggests, as a result of his well-publicized disagreements with Walesa over the plans for the commemoration.

Avi Weiss was at Auschwitz once again, this time staging a sit-in in the parish church of Brzezinka and complaining that the ceremonies that had been organized had emphasized a Polish memory of Auschwitz at the expense of the Jewish memory. The EJC was organizing its own ceremony – whether it was a 'counter-ceremony' or a 'supplementary ceremony' was open to interpretation. In short, it was 'business as usual'.

12. Winter 1997–98 to Winter 1999:
Will It Stay or Will It Go?

Another commemoration the following year was also tinged with controversy. Elie Wiesel was again invited to Poland, this time to speak on the fiftieth anniversary of the Kielce pogrom on 7 July 1996. Besides pointing out that the pogrom proved that anti-Semitism in Poland had not died with Auschwitz, Wiesel protested strongly against religious symbols being placed on the field of ashes in Birkenau.

For once it was not the large papal cross that was the subject of contention. The 'religious symbols' – small crosses and small wooden Stars of David – had been placed in Birkenau several years earlier when the site was cleared by a group of young people from Warsaw. These symbols were undoubtedly placed there as a gesture of goodwill and, contrary to their policy of refusing to sanction any private symbols of commemoration, the Auschwitz museum authorities had allowed a number to remain. It appears that some more ambiguous crosses with a 'crucified' Star of David had been placed there too. These, however, were soon removed.

Not many visitors to Auschwitz would have been familiar with these crosses and stars since the field of ashes is located far from the entrance to the Birkenau camp. Most of the victims whose ashes were strewn there were Hungarian Jews murdered in 1944. For Wiesel, whose own family was scattered among these victims, the crosses were 'an insult'. Jews, he explained, did not need to erect Stars of David or any other symbols.

As Stanislaw Krajewski pointed out in a chapter from his book *Jews, Judaism, Poland*, the furore over the crosses provoked by Wiesel's speech 'overshadowed the issue of the pogrom and the moral challenge it presented'. However, it was more than a year later that the subject of the offending religious symbols was formally raised at a meeting of the Auschwitz Museum Council in October 1997. The Council voted to urge the Polish minister of culture to remove the symbols.

To avoid an anti-Semitic backlash, the Council worked discretely and made sure that the Church had no objection to the removal of the crosses. Finally in February 1998 eight crosses and 11 Stars of David were removed, under orders from the Polish government. The crosses were given to a local church and the Stars of David to a Jewish archive in Cracow. 'This is a great achievement', Kalman Sultanik, a vice-president of the Auschwitz Museum Council as well as the WJC, told the *WJC International Report*. 'I think this will be a step in the improvement of Polish–Jewish relations.'

The removal of the religious symbols was one condition the Holocaust Memorial Council had imposed before agreeing to co-operate with the Polish government on a master plan for Auschwitz–Birkenau. The document outlining the plan had originally been presented some years earlier to Miles Lerman, president of the Holocaust Museum in Washington, by Polish President Kwasniewski on a visit to the museum. Lerman had co-opted other Jewish movements, including the WJC, and some non-Jewish experts into the process.

Even before the crosses and Stars of David were removed, negotiations for the transfer of the large papal cross had finally begun. At that stage no one was to know that rather than receive a further boost, Polish–Jewish relations were once again to be challenged by a furore that would echo the sound and fury expended over the Carmelite convent.

It would be ironic to presume that a gesture from the Carmelites might have precipitated moves towards a possible solution of the papal cross controversy. However, a *Jewish Chronicle* report of 3 April stated that 'last month Carmelite nuns gave the land with the cross to the state'. This, apparently, had led to an announcement from the Polish government and Church that they were seeking a compromise with Jewish groups. The government's proposal to replace the cross with a smaller religious symbol was endorsed by Bishop Stanislaw Gadecki, head of the Polish Church's committee for dialogue with Judaism, who suggested replacing the cross with a smaller monument incorporating the image of a cross.

These compromise proposals failed to find favour with many in the higher echelons of the Polish state and Church. The primate, Cardinal Glemp, for one, took issue with the idea of moving the cross. The cross 'cannot be a subject of bargaining', he pronounced in a sermon on 22 March. 'Many have not liked the Eiffel Tower but that is no reason to move it or tinker with it'. Glemp's harder line was echoed by war veterans and politicians, including former President Lech Walesa. Some 140 deputies, mainly from the Solidarity bloc, signed a letter of protest against the removal of the cross.

The opposing point of view was forcefully expressed by Polish Chief Rabbi Menachem Joskowicz, who urged Catholic leaders to remove the cross. 'It disturbs my prayers. How did I sin that I cannot pray in the holy place where my family died, where my nation died', he declared in an impassioned radio interview.

In a more diplomatic vein Stanislaw Krajewski, too, contended that the cross was not best situated in a place that had become a symbol of the extermination of the Jews. He suggested that its removal would be in accordance with the spirit of the recent Vatican document 'We Remember: A Reflection on the Shoah'. Indeed at a meeting at the Vatican to discuss the document, the International Catholic–Jewish Liaison Committee, co-chaired by Cardinal Cassidy and Gerhart Riegner, issued a joint communiqué recommending the transfer of the cross to a site away from the camp.

As Jewish protests about the cross continued, Bishop Tadeusz Pieronek, secretary of the Polish bishops' conference, expressed the hope that the cross would not become 'the cause of division and hatred' since it was a sign of martyrdom and love. In a radio interview he recalled the removal of crosses by totalitarian regimes. 'The removal of a cross is a terrible thing. It is the height of intolerance', he said. Although the decision about the Auschwitz cross was a matter for the local church authorities, he believed it should remain 'for the moment'.

In the midst of the renewed conflict over the future of the cross, Israeli Prime Minister, Binyamin Netanyahu, headed the biggest-ever 'March of the Living' from Auschwitz to Birkenau in April 1998. The march along the two-mile route from the gates of Auschwitz bearing the slogan *Arbeit Macht Frei* to the gas chambers of Birkenau was initiated on Holocaust Memorial Day 1990. Each year thousands of young Jews, accompanied by Holocaust survivors, joined together to make the symbolic journey.

Now, a week before Israel's fiftieth anniversary, Netanyahu used the occasion to proclaim the importance of the Jewish state: 'This is the lesson of the Holocaust, this and only this: that the existence of the Jewish people is tied to Jewish sovereignty and a Jewish army that rests on the strength of the Jewish faith.'

Also on the march was Israel's Ashkenazi Chief Rabbi, Israel Meir Lau, himself a survivor of Auschwitz. 'Despite the difficulties and plans of the past we are still here, not on a death march but a living one', he said. 'For me, there is a double thank you to the Almighty, for my personal survival and for the gift he has given me to see this fiftieth anniversary of the State of Israel.'

The year 1998 was the first in which Polish Jews had been invited on the march. However, as Stanislaw Krajewski remarked, the Polish language was not used at all, although French and Spanish were, as well as English and 'the dominant Hebrew'. While welcoming the idea of the march, Krajewski had mixed feelings about it, in part because Polish Jews had previously been excluded. More importantly, he believed it has been exploited by Israelis to score political points and has perpetuated an 'us and them' mentality, with Poles often distinguished as the prime villains among 'them' – the perpetrators.

Another event in upbeat mode was an international interfaith conference on 'Religion and Violence, Religion and Peace' sponsored by the Centre for Information, Meetings, Dialogue, Education and Prayer at Auschwitz the following month. The Centre, so long something of a white elephant, brought together 30 religious leaders of the three Abrahamic faiths, Christians, Muslims and Jews, from 12 countries.

The American orthodox rabbi, Joseph Ehrenkrantz, Director of the Centre for Christian–Jewish Understanding at the Sacred Heart University in Fairfield, Connecticut, praised Catholic attempts to understand Jews and singled out Cardinal Franciszek Macharski as one of the churchmen who had shown a deep desire to work with Jews. 'From the Jewish point of view it is hardly believable that the Catholic Church is still accused of indifference to Jewish concerns', said Ehrenkrantz, an organizer of the conference and one of five orthodox rabbis from Israel and America to take part. As well as a number of cardinals, the conference was attended by Father Remi Hoeckman, secretary of the Vatican commission for relations with Judaism.

The positive impact generated by the March of the Living and the interfaith conference was sadly fleeting. These were glimpses of light on a horizon that was becoming ever more stormy.

13. Spring 1998 to Early Summer 1999:
Defender of the Cross

The intimation that the papal cross might be relocated had provoked a particularly extreme reaction from a group of militant Catholics. Led by Kazimierz Switon, formerly a leader of the free trade union movement among the Katowice miners in the late 1970s, the 'defenders of the cross' won the support of Miecyslaw Janosz, Chairman of the Polish War Victims Association, who was leasing the former convent building. Switon, in fact, was given the key to the property, ostensibly so that he might allow pilgrims to come in. On 11 June, the day after the celebration of Corpus Christi, he began a fast 'in defence of the cross', as tensions over the future of the cross continued to rise.

In the meantime, the Polish government had initialled the working document for the master plan for Auschwitz–Birkenau and a signing ceremony was scheduled in Warsaw in early July. With a new government in office, this seemed a particularly propitious time. A few days before the scheduled date, however, a pronouncement by Kalman Sultanik that Auschwitz–Birkenau should be taken out of Polish hands and internationalized ensured that the signing ceremony would not go ahead. Elie Wiesel also came out against the signing and other organizations followed suit.

With negotiations over the future of Auschwitz at stalemate, Switon terminated his 42-day fast at the request of Archbishop Kazimierz Majdanski of Szczecin-Kamien. 'I have suspended my fast, since, as a Catholic, I must obey the bishops', Switon said. As reported in *The Tablet*, he added that he had received assurances that the church authorities would try to arrange that the papal cross remained.

In his statement Switon appealed to the Polish public to bring small crosses to erect around the large cross, making it a 'valley of crosses'. By the end of the day, 50 small crosses had been erected close to the papal cross. He also called for fasts and prayers to be organized at parish level in defence of the cross.

As Polish emotions grew ever more inflamed over the issue, a Citizen's Committee for the Defence of the Auschwitz Cross was established, basing its stance on the words of the Pope who, in a homily at Zakopane during his last visit to Poland, had urged the congregation to 'defend the cross'. According to *The Tablet*, however, whether the Pontiff had this particular controversial cross in mind was open to question.

By the first week of August, the Jewish world had stepped in. Rabbi Avi Weiss announced that he intended to travel to Poland to protest against the crosses. And Israeli authorities issued a complaint to the government of Poland, demanding the removal of the crosses which, they said, were 'an affront to the Jewish victims of the Holocaust'.

The Polish government responded by stating that since religious symbols were involved it was a matter for the Catholic Church to decide. An article in the London Polish weekly *Tydzien Polski* of 8 August quoted the head of the Polish prime minister's office as remarking sardonically that, 'Maybe there should be no crosses in the vicinity of Auschwitz, even in Oswiecim or Brzezinka, if this offends Jewish sensibilities'. The official went on to remark that he was expecting 'our Jewish friends to respect the feelings of Catholics'.

The fate of the papal cross was the responsibility of the local bishop, Tadeusz Rakoczy. While he wished all the crosses to be removed, he was unable to react, as he told the Polish Press Agency, because all this was now beyond his control. 'It is not known what circles, on what inspiration and why they do this. One can hardly forbid doing that because no one would respect it.' Rakoczy was not optimistic about chances for a compromise over the crosses as so many people were engaged in the action.

The altercation also provoked further intervention from Cardinal Glemp. The crosses should remain in place, he said, to mark the deaths of many Christians who perished in the camp. 'The land is Polish and for any other will to be imposed on it would be interference in its state affairs.'

Calling for 'calm reflection' in response to the controversy, Glemp said the cross was a symbol for all Christians, not only Catholics. It was 'accepted and recognized in Western civilization as a sign of loving sacrifice and suffering'. Referring to Switon and his followers, however, the primate's rhetoric grew more heightened: 'In the name of truth, it is necessary to say that this team ... [arose] ... as a result of constant and increasing harassment from the Jewish side for the earliest possible removal of the crosses', he declared, concluding, however, that he hoped the quarrel might be 'exploited for the process of accord'.

By the following week, Glemp had softened his stance, even backtracking on his earlier remarks about Jewish provocation. This was probably as a result of representations made to the Vatican by inter-

faith activists, including Sternberg, who argued that dialogue and consultation were the only means to resolve the dispute between Catholic
sensibilities and legitimate Jewish fears. Without calling for the existing crosses to be removed, the Cardinal asked the militant Catholic
defenders of the cross to stop erecting any more crosses at the site. 'I
appeal to all interested parties to stop placing the crosses', he said in
a letter to Polish bishops.

Other Church dignitaries took a less ambiguous line. Archbishop
Henryk Muszynski, now the primate's deputy, said that erecting
crosses was a blow to the dignity of the Church and the Christian symbol of the cross, while Archbishop Tadeusz Goclowski of Gdansk called
for all but the papal cross to be removed. Goclowski criticized the
Church for not making its position clear.

By now the Oswiecim council had given notice to Janosz to terminate
the lease, provoking Janosz to take his case to court. On 18 August the
Polish government issued a statement saying it would ask the court to
declare that the gravel pit at the Auschwitz camp was state property
since the War Victims Association had flouted the terms of the lease to
uphold the 'sacral character' of the property. The government added
that it accepted the arguments of the local bishop, Tadeusz Rakoczy,
that the placing of crosses had violated the Church's authority.

Not surprisingly the government's move was rejected by Janosz
and by Switon who, as reported in the London daily *Dziennik Polski*, had
suddenly appeared in court. Switon protested that the regional court
in which the case was being tried was not competent to try a case
involving culture and religion which should be the preserve of the
provincial court of Bielsko-Biala. While the court did not accept Switon's
assertion, it nevertheless turned down the government's request to
evict the War Victims Association.

After the case, Adam Bielski, manager of the regional council of
Oswiecim, said he would lodge a complaint against the court's decision.
Bielski also appealed to the police to prevent the placing of any more
crosses in the gravel pit. By now at least 100 crosses had been erected
and Switon was appealing to supporters to place more three-meter
crosses by the end of the week in memory of the 152 Polish prisoners
executed at the gravel pit.

This incitement to put up crosses was extended to Catholics abroad
through Radio Maryja, an independent Catholic radio station that
broadcast and raised funds in the United States. Not satisfied with
merely defending the papal cross, the act of erecting crosses was seen
as part of 'a holy war against alleged Jewish conspiracies, the government, the West and anyone who disagrees with their interpretation of
God's word' waged by nationalist Polish Catholic priests. As reported

in the *Sunday Telegraph*, even conservative Roman Catholics had been 'irked' by the message and tone of the broadcasts. An observer from England, Chris Schwarz, has also noted that broadcasts from Radio Maryja were relayed at full volume whenever groups of Jews were visiting Auschwitz.

In the meantime Israel's two chief rabbis had appealed to the Pope to intervene. In a joint letter of 18 August delivered via the St Egidio Community, Rabbi Israel Meir Lau and Rabbi Eliahu Bakshi-Doron urged the Pope to ensure the crosses were withdrawn, in order that future generations should not be 'led into error' by a 'Christian re-reading of history'. At the same time Archbishop Muszynski had criticized attempts by the 'defenders of the cross' to invoke the Pope's authority for their actions as a 'clear distortion' of John Paul II's real intentions.

A meeting of the Polish Bishops' Conference was scheduled for the following week and was expected to call for the removal of the crosses while defending the setting up of the original papal cross. In its wake, a special emergency session was arranged by Sternberg at Erlbach in Germany during the annual consultation of the International Council of Christians and Jews.

At the Erlbach session, the Polish bishops' statement was reviewed by Stanislaw Krajewski. The bishops had declared that since the cross was being used as an instrument of strife all the new crosses were seen as a provocation and should be removed and relocated in parishes. As far as the papal cross was concerned, however, the bishops 'stated [their] belief that it will remain'. Although, as Krajewski acknowledged, the papal cross was also erected in a spirit of defiance, it was difficult to refute the argument that it memorialized the murder in 1941 of the Polish Catholic resistance fighters. Moreover, in an effort to respect Jewish sensibilities the bishops had also declared that they were open to dialogue 'as to how to shape the greatest cemetery of our time'.

Another speaker at the emergency session at Erlbach was the Catholic theologian, Father John Pawlikowski, who, among his other activities, was a member of the Holocaust Memorial Council. Pawlikowski welcomed the bishops' statement as an opening for negotiation but emphasized the importance of getting discussions for the master plan for Auschwitz–Birkenau back on track. While it was a priority to ensure the removal of the new crosses, the papal cross, he believed, was 'the Jerusalem issue' and should be left to the end of the negotiations.

The Erlbach panel, which included Cardinal Cassidy and Sternberg himself, also discussed various suggestions for appropriate memorials for all victims. It was agreed that the current crisis should be handled by the Polish government and the Catholic bishops without outside interference. If they failed to reach a satisfactory resolution, then the Vatican should intercede, as it had done previously.

While the bishops' appeal was rejected by Switon, who demanded 'written assurance' from Church and government leaders that the 'papal cross' would stay in perpetuity, it was welcomed by Sultanik of the WJC as a 'very important step forward'. Already on 11 August a coalition of Jewish organizations in America had held a critical meeting at which it was decided to exercise patience and give the Polish side one month to resolve the problem of removing the crosses.

In reply, as reported in *Dziennik Polski* of 4 September, the Polish prime minister and several bishops, including Glemp and Muszynski, had sent a letter to Miles Lerman, president of the Washington Holocaust Museum, in an attempt to convince the 16 Jewish organizations that the Polish government and Church had every intention of finding a solution to the crisis.

It appeared that the case of the crosses was of particular concern in American Catholic circles. On the one hand, American bishops and leaders of the religious community were afraid that the Polish situation could damage the dialogue between the American Church and Judaism which was supported by the Pope and to which Church leaders attached great importance. On another level it was believed that if the situation was not resolved quickly and the crosses removed, there would be loud protests in America against the profanation of the cross since the crosses were being used in the place of banners of political protest.

The greatest worry the Polish situation held for American Catholics, according to the report in *Dziennik Polski*, centred on the disregard of Church authority displayed by Switon and his followers as well as other Poles. This, it was feared, might lead to a schism in Poland, a country which had been faithful to Rome for 1000 years. Such an eventuality would be particularly tragic during the papacy of a Pole. In this context the pilgrimage to Auschwitz of the schismatic brothers of the late renegade French Archbishop Lefebvre was seen as particularly disturbing.

Another controversial figure to come out in support of the crosses was the Gdansk priest, Father Henryk Jankowski, currently under suspension for his previous anti-Semitic outbursts. He urged Catholics to defend the crosses and ensure that Poles were not made 'a minority in their own country'.

In opposition to these moves the Polish government continued to pursue its case against Janosz and the War Victims Association in a bid to repossess the gravel pit. At this point the district court of Oswiecim, which had earlier upheld Janosz's appeal to remain at the old theatre building, reversed its decision and ordered him to leave. According to

Dziennik Polski of 21 October, this later decision was harmful to Polish interests since it prolonged the conflict surrounding the gravel pit. Defending his decision the judge had pointed out the seriousness of the problem and the grievance this could cause. By now there were 238 'Switon' crosses surrounding the Papal cross.

It was clear that the Polish government was concerned at the negative influence the Auschwitz cross controversy was causing to Poland's image abroad. This was conveyed to Sternberg when he visited Warsaw in November at the invitation of the Polish government. Polish President Kwasniewski, who had expressed disquiet about the failure of those who had planted the 'field of crosses' to remove them, told Sternberg of proposals under consideration that might ameliorate the situation.

At a tea-time visit with the president, with the British ambassador also present, Sternberg told Kwasniewski that similar situations might be avoided in the future if a task force were established consisting of a member of the government and Jewish and Christian representatives.

He went further in an address given at Warsaw University on 4 November, declaring that Auschwitz was not a place for a war of religion, 'of Cross against Star of David, of rabbi against priest, of Christian against Jew ... It needs no symbols, especially when they are placed in such a manner as to serve not as a memorial but as a provocation ... Auschwitz does not need a "selection process" which seems to suggest that one religion's dead are more worthy than another.' Sternberg hoped that the symbols would be removed 'quietly with dignity and their place taken by a simple monument which records the men, women and children who died there as martyrs'.

As the year ended with no solution in sight, the WJC issued a statement in Jerusalem reviewing the current standing of Catholic–Jewish relations. Among Vatican decisions criticized by the WJC for shifting relations between the faiths into reverse gear was its 'inactive response' to the erection of crucifixes at Auschwitz.

In February 1999, Archbishop Henryk Muszynski, referred to by Stanislaw Krajewski in a letter to Sternberg as 'our only friend', paid a brief visit to London where he met with Sternberg. Muszynski was to receive the Buber-Rosenzweig prize in Germany the following month for promoting relations between Poles, Jews and Germans. In anticipation of his visit to London, Krajewski wrote to Sternberg hoping that some clarity might emerge with regard to the gravel pit crisis in conversations with the archbishop.

Krajewski's letter reported an increase in manifestations of anti-Semitism in Poland. These included the vandalizing of tombstones and, for the first time, the appearance of Polish Holocaust-denial publications, all attributable to the 'deterioration of the social atmosphere' caused by the cross conflict.

Although Krajewski had hoped for some backing from the Polish Church in driving through a resolution and had even suggested that force might be necessary, Muszynski indicated that both the Church and the Polish government were powerless to push. It appeared that the Janosz case was now in the hands of an independent court that refused to bow to outside influence, even though they were aware that the matter had become an international affair. Muszynski suggested that one reason for the court's caution was that Janosz himself was a lawyer.

By the end of April, however, the Polish parliament had passed legislation restricting activities outside former Nazi concentration camps. As reported by the Catholic News Service of 23 April, gatherings, building projects and non-essential commerce would be barred from a 100-metre zone around Auschwitz–Birkenau and other Nazi camps.

With regard to religious symbols there was some disagreement between the Sejm, the lower house, and the Senate. Doubtless with the 'field of crosses' in mind, a deputy interior minister said the legislation, while not affecting activities by local churches or religious groups, would enable the government 'to prevent acts of extremists on various sides whose activity damages the good name and interests of Poland and the Poles'. This legislation was amended by the Senate to allow religious symbols accepted by the churches. The papal cross, for example, would be allowed to stay. In a debate on the amendment, a member of the Sejm's Internal Affairs Commission urged parliamentarians to reject it on the grounds that it could lead to 'some unknown religious association' stating that it agreed to the placing of hundreds of crosses at Auschwitz – 'and they would have to stay'. However a spokesman for the Polish bishops' conference told the *Gazeta Wyborcza* that the Senate amendment was a step in the right direction. The timing for removing the crosses from Auschwitz would be decided by the local bishop, he said.

14. May 1999 to Summer 2000:
Compromise or Retreat?

The passing of the new law establishing the 100-metre protection zone turned out to be one crucial factor in the eventual resolution of the crisis. The other major factor was the imminence of a papal visit to Poland, scheduled for 5 to 17 June. This is likely to have had the same effect on the long drawn-out dispute over the crosses as the looming Warsaw Ghetto Uprising commemoration had had on the eventual transfer of the Carmelites six years earlier.

Switon's response to the new legislation was to demand the opening of a chapel on the site of the former convent as a condition for the removal of over 300 crosses. He again insisted on legal guarantees that the 'papal cross' would be allowed to remain permanently. His statement was welcomed by Bishop Gadecki of the committee for dialogue with Judaism, who claimed that several Jewish groups had agreed to the possibility of an interfaith prayer centre in the 'old theatre' building.

The Polish government, however, was in no mood to accede to Switon's conditions. A representative made it clear that Church leaders would be consulted about how to remove the 300 crosses in the run-up to the Pope's visit and that a final decision on the gravel pit would be taken by local government authorities. 'We are determined to take over the site, restore its serious character and ensure that all crosses except the papal one are removed', she said. The popular *Gazeta Wyborcza* warned that opening a place of worship at the old theatre would 'guarantee not peace but a new Polish–Jewish war'.

Although Switon appeared in court on 10 May on charges of slander in connection with the circulation of anti-Semitic leaflets at Auschwitz, his followers were not deterred. Three more crosses were erected during a mass on 23 May in the face of disciplinary threats by Church leaders. There was also further vandalism in Jewish cemeteries at Cracow and Tarnow.

As the papal visit drew nearer, it seemed clear that the cross John Paul II had used at the mass at Birkenau 20 years earlier was not under threat, even if no legal guarantee to that effect had been provided.

Nevertheless, Switon was becoming increasingly desperate. In a bid to prevent the removal of the smaller crosses, he planted explosives and detonators in the gravel pit in a last-ditch action that helped provide justification for the dramatic operation that was about to take place.

In a dawn raid on Friday, 28 May, hundreds of Polish policemen and troops swooped on Auschwitz, detonated the devices in controlled explosions, and removed the more than 300 crosses. These were taken to a Franciscan monastery in Oswiecim where they were placed on the ground to be claimed by the people who had erected them. Any unclaimed crosses were to be re-erected in the monastery grounds. The police also arrested Switon, who was to face charges in connection with the explosives. In January 2000, he was convicted by the court in Oswiecim for inciting hatred against Jews and given a suspended sentence.

The Polish government's initiative in removing the crosses was hailed in many quarters. Welcoming the move in a statement to the *Jewish Chronicle*, Sternberg took a sober and remarkably prescient line in relation to the papal cross, suggesting that trees should be planted at the site if the cross were to remain in place.

The removal of the 'Switon crosses' was also welcomed by Jerzy Kichler, head of Poland's Jewish community, as 'a step in the right direction'. However he stressed that the Jewish community was waiting for the papal cross to be removed as well. 'We believe there should be no religious symbols at Auschwitz', he said, 'not because we have a negative attitude to the cross but because Jewish tradition does not allow us to pray for our dead relatives in the presence of symbols belonging to another religion'.

The same argument was expressed more dramatically, if inappropriately, by Chief Rabbi Joskowicz. At a ceremony in June at the Umschlagplatz in Warsaw where Pope John Paul II was praying in memory of the Jewish victims of the *Shoah*, Joskowicz begged the Pontiff to intervene to remove the remaining papal cross at Auschwitz. 'I would like to ask the Pope to urge his people to take the last cross out of the camp so that Jews who come here can say their final prayer before dying', he said. The Pope made no response.

As well as embarrassing many Polish Jews, Joskowicz may well have offended Polish Catholic feelings. However a high court inquiry into the incident the following month found that the rabbi had not offended the religious feelings of the Polish nation or committed any offence. Nevertheless, it was the end of his long career. He was dismissed from his position as chief rabbi and replaced by a young Lubavich rabbi from Russia. Before long, however, the new rabbi resigned of his own accord and at the time of writing Poland has no chief rabbi.

The Joskowicz incident as well as the removal of the crosses may well have fuelled the climate of anti-Semitism to which Krajewski had often referred. Indeed, on a visit to her former homeland in the autumn, a Polish lady remarked on a wall emblazoned with the words '*Juden Raus*' in the centre of her home town of Przemysl. She also recalled seeing graffiti proclaiming '*Zydzi do Gasu*' – Jews to the gas [chambers] – while on a train journey in Poland in 1992, at the height of the convent dispute.

On the official level, however, Polish–Jewish relations remained unscathed. In May, Jonathan Webber had been awarded the Gold Cross of the Order of Merit of the President of the Republic of Poland for his contribution to Polish–Jewish dialogue. Then in October, Sternberg received his third Polish award, the Commander's Cross with a Star of the Order of Merit.

In a speech at the award ceremony at the Polish embassy in London, Sternberg focused on how best to preserve and hallow Auschwitz–Birkenau, 'made holy by the blood and ashes of our kinsfolk, Polish and Jewish'. Once again he praised the Polish government for removing 'the field of crosses' which had been placed at the concentration camp 'not as a statement of faith or of memorial, but as a deliberate provocation'.

Sternberg also referred to a recent report that a discotheque was to be opened in a warehouse near the camp where the Nazis had stored the hair of their victims. This was something to which he – and his many listeners – 'reacted with horror'. Fortunately this very inappropriate project was later dropped. The proposal was the latest and the most disconcerting of many which had been put forward over the years for the commercialization of the area surrounding the camp.

This was a question of which Sternberg was well aware. He warned against Auschwitz becoming something of a 'Disneyland of tragedy'. 'Auschwitz–Birkenau should be looked upon as a challenge to the planners and environmentalists of the world to come up with a setting worthy of this terrible and unique memorial to the millions of Europe's murdered innocents', he said.

Negotiations towards this end were proceeding quietly between the Polish government and Jewish organizations throughout the world. Nevertheless news of an agreement about the papal cross may have surprised some followers of the protracted Auschwitz saga. A report in *Dziennik Polski* of 8 November said that the Polish government had accepted an agreement with Jewish organizations in Israel, the USA and Europe and with representatives of the Roma that the papal cross should stay. The same news was reported in a brief footnote in the *Jewish Chronicle* of 19 November, while a report in *The Tablet* of

27 November entitled 'Auschwitz's "War of the Crosses" Ends' made no reference to the agreement about the papal cross. Instead the report focused on a ruling by the regional court at Oswiecim that the gravel pit should be handed back to its rightful owner, the state treasury.

Had *Dziennik Polski* and the sources from which it derived its information jumped the gun? Certainly many interested parties, both Jewish and non-Jewish, remained ignorant of the so-called agreement and a concerted effort to discover who exactly had been involved met, for a long time, with little or no response.

In a faxed reply to the author in April 2000, Kalman Sultanik, Chairman of the American Section of the World Zionist Organisation, a Vice-President of the WJC and a member of the International Auschwitz Council, recalled a conference call at the US Holocaust Memorial Museum in Washington with the participation of Agnieszka Magdziak-Miszewska from the Polish prime minister's office. The majority of people in the conference call, Sultanik remarked, had reached the agreement the author had described. He was unable to recall, however, who the participants had been.

Sultanik, nevertheless, was asked whether he would agree to the papal cross remaining in Auschwitz 'under specific physical conditions, such as being blocked by trees'. He replied that he would have to read the full agreement 'before deciding whether to go along with it or not'. The agreement, however, was never received in his office. A similar proposal for 'screening' was brought up by Cardinal Glemp during a private meeting in London with Sir Sigmund Sternberg. Sternberg was of the opinion that the proposal warranted consideration.

Who exactly had been party to the agreement remained a moot point. According to Withold Sobkow, Minister Plenipotentiary at the Polish embassy in London, Jewish organizations outside Poland had not been involved in the agreement. This had been reached between the Polish government and certain members of the International Auschwitz Council.

The Council was disbanded in January 2000 but reformed under the same name with a greatly expanded brief in June the same year. Returning from the inaugural meeting of the newly reconstituted Council, Jonathan Webber, a founder member, gave the author further details of the agreement which did, indeed, state that the papal cross could remain *in situ* provided it was 'screened off'. It appears that pine trees have already been planted to provide the 'screening'. Webber is not impressed by the compromise, however, finding the 'prettiness' of the trees far more distasteful than the presence of the cross.

Others are more enthusiastic. 'We'll have the cross surrounded by trees', the author was told by Miles Lerman, President of the US

Holocaust Memorial Museum, at the Remembering for the Future conference in July 2000. Negotiations were still continuing, Lerman said, intimating that a resolution was expected within the following three months. Lerman confirmed, too, that in addition to the International Auschwitz Council, Jewish organizations worldwide were still involved in the negotiations, as *Dziennik Polski* had reported. These organizations include the Anti-Defamation League, the American Jewish Congress, the World Jewish Congress, the European Jewish Congress and Yad Vashem – in short, many of the leading players in the long-running saga.

For a conflict involving such *Sturm und Drang* to end with barely a whimper leaves much to the arts of speculation. Rather than being trumpeted as a victory for dialogue and compromise, the decision to allow the papal cross to remain leaves the Jewish world licking its wounds.

A more positive outcome of the drama is the restoration of the only surviving synagogue at Oswiecim and the creation there of a Jewish Centre for Study, Prayer and Information. The $10 million project, conceived and sponsored by the New York Auschwitz Jewish Centre Foundation, fulfils many of the aspirations of the 'Jewish House at Oswiecim' which Jonathan Webber had proposed years earlier. The aims of the centre are to commemorate the victims by showing how they lived, not how they died, and to establish a living Jewish presence in the place that has become the ultimate symbol of the *Shoah*.

At the ground-breaking ceremony in November 1999, Holocaust survivors were joined by Roman Catholic clergy and Polish, American and Israeli officials. Bishop Rakoczy was there, as was former Knesset Speaker Shevach Weiss. A Holocaust survivor blew the *shofar* and Jonathan Webber led *Kaddish* and other prayers. As Stanislaw Krajewski told a *Jewish Chronicle* reporter: 'Everybody from the Polish government to the US ambassador, to the Polish Jews, to the Polish Church, is happy that it is possible to do something constructive at Auschwitz.'

A similar positive note was struck by Prince Hassan of Jordan who, as the *Jewish Chronicle* reported, was present when the synagogue was officially consecrated in September 2000. 'There is in today's ceremony a message of hope, of *tikvah*,' the prince said. 'After survival comes revival: the message here is that death is not the end of life.'

Afterword

While it might seem flippant to compare the 15-year 'Battle for Auschwitz' with the proverbial Shakesperian 'tale told by an idiot, full of sound and fury, signifying nothing', the deafening silence from the Jewish world in the wake of the agreement over Auschwitz's papal cross tells its own story.

And yet, and here lies the paradox, as Judith Banki of the Tanenbaum Foundation in New York aptly observed, the controversy 'had everything in it: clashes of historic memory; conflicts of religious and ethnic identity, particularly between Jews and Polish Catholics; unreconciled views on how the suffering of these victimized people should be memorialized'. There was, as Banki remarked, 'a pervasive sense of some advancing menace and of powerlessness to stop it'. These remarks in an essay in *Memory Offended* in 1991 strike me, a mere chronicler of events, as particularly pertinent, even nine years later.

For Sternberg, the main lesson to be drawn from the long struggle, which he considers was badly handled and during which 'so much bad blood and so much energy was wasted', is the importance of frank and open dialogue in dealing with sensitive issues to prevent disagreement from turning into dispute.

Indeed, at its best, dialogue can lead to greater empathy, as expressed by Father Stanislaw Musial, one of the Geneva signatories, in a recent interview in a Chicago Polish newspaper. 'Auschwitz is the symbol of the Holocaust and should join us, Jews and Catholics, in grief and compassion instead of being a source of so much hatred,' he said. Musial, who had witnessed Jewish suffering as a boy in wartime Poland, was also quoted as saying that he felt so close to Jews that he wanted *Kaddish* said for him when he died.

It is unlikely that many Jews can evince the same sensitivity regarding the importance to Christians of the Cross. And in the case of the papal cross at Auschwitz, put up in a spirit of defiance, this is, perhaps, understandable. Yet the cross remains, in perpetuity – the cross that was erected, as it were, 'in defence of the convent' and was itself 'defended' by the erection of the 'field of crosses'. Essentially, it can be seen as a victory for Sister Teresa, a 'battle-axe', as Sternberg has called her, against whom the pitted might of world Jewry and well-meaning liberal Catholicism proved impotent.

As I see it, the Mother Superior was essentially a strategist. And what the Jewish world has lacked throughout the conflict is strategy. It has relied on the empathy of highly educated and sensitive Catholics like Musial, an empathy also expressed in some articles in *The Tablet* during the height of the furore over the crosses. These acknowledged the misuse of the cross in 'the largest Jewish cemetery' and saw silence as the only fitting memorial.

Such sentiments are in tune with majority Jewish opinion which cherishes the concept of Auschwitz as a desolate space left to decay. However Auschwitz is in Poland where Jewish opinion is, at best, marginal. The Jewish world, therefore, has had to learn the hard way that it has little control over what others wish to do at the site of the death camps, be it erect memorials or crosses or open tourist facilities. One such example is the construction of a shopping centre near Auschwitz sanctioned by the Polish interior ministry during the summer of 2000 after the World Jewish Congress had forced building work to a halt. But even the Polish government was powerless to stop a discotheque opening the same summer just outside the legally protected zone around the death camp.

As a first step, the Jewish world will need to come to terms with the cross now that it is to remain permanently at Auschwitz. While I have never been to Auschwitz and have no personal impression of the cross, I have questioned people who have visited recently, including Geoffrey Paul, former editor of the *Jewish Chronicle*, as to how it affected them. The unanimous verdict, to my surprise, was very little. One lady had made a point of seeking out the cross on my behalf and reported that she had to go to the first floor of the museum in order to see it. These views are very different from those I have quoted in the text which speak of the cross dominating the landscape.

On another level, it may be time for Jews to reassess their perception of the Cross as a symbol of anti-Semitism 'second only to the swastika', as Clifford Longley pointed out in an article in the *Daily Telegraph* in August 1998, while the battle of the crosses raged on. Calling for 'honest dialogue' between Christians and Jews about the meaning of the Cross, Longley made an important – and for Jews novel – observation. The Cross, he explained, has 'represented sorrow: sorrow at Christ's death and sorrow for sin (sorrow, therefore, for the sin of anti-Semitism, too)'.

Another interpretation of the Cross has been made by a few

contemporary Christian theologians, Alice Eckhardt for one. This is
to visualize the crucified Jesus suffering with his people in the death
camps, as in the Chagall painting. An even more radical interpretation
is to view the Jewish people, 'the Christ among the nations', suffering
crucifixion in the Nazi *Shoah*. With this in mind, some Jews consider
the cross an appropriate symbol at Auschwitz while others have even
voiced support for a cross bearing a Star of David.

These interpretations are admittedly controversial and may give
offence to many Jews. As Stanislaw Krajewski argued in *Jews, Judaism,
Poland*, by comparing the *Shoah* with the sufferings of Jesus, sympathetic Christians are regarding it as a kind of sacrifice offered on
an altar, thereby ennobling the perpetrators of the 'sacrifice': 'The
Christian interpretation attributes more meaning to the martyrdom
in gas chambers than it is possible for most Jews to accept.'

Even were Jews to come to accept the presence of the cross in
Auschwitz, this is only the beginning. What the 'Battle for Auschwitz'
has demonstrated most clearly is the need for the Jewish world not
merely to litigate against the actions and interests of others but to do
something constructive for itself.

Like Judith Banki, Rabbi Marc Tanenbaum had raised the subject
of 'how the victims of Nazism should be memorialized'. The March of
the Living which, in future, will be open to non-Jews, is one means of
enabling 'anyone to be present and reflect from his/her point of view
about the tragedy, one's own connection to it, and to participate in
the celebration that, despite everything, *Am Israel hai*'. Here I quote
Krajewski. And certainly, as he has pointed out, the ruins of the
crematoria serve as a focal point and 'monument'.

But with the papal cross serving as a permanent memorial for the
martyred Poles and the ruins of the crematoria liable to decay, is not
the need for a specifically Jewish monument at Auschwitz now greater
than ever? Over ten years ago, Jonathan Webber had already recommended a Jewish memorial. He was, of course, more familiar than
most Western Jews with the reality of Auschwitz today. Not only is a
memorial needed to bear witness to future generations of the greatest catastrophe in the history of the Jewish diaspora. It is needed to
ensure, as Webber has often pointed out, that Auschwitz is 'sacralized'
from a Jewish point of view.

The challenge now for world Jewry is to to make its own imprint on
Auschwitz as a mark of respect for the site of what is in fact the largest
Jewish cemetery in the world.